State College

YOU CAN'T
DO IT
ALL

YOU CAN'T DO IT ALL

Ideas That Work for Mothers Who Work

Irvina Siegel Lew

ATHENEUM *New York*
1986

Library of Congress Cataloging-in-Publication Data

Lew, Irvina Siegel.
You can't do it all.

1. Mothers—United States—Time management.
2. Children of working mothers—United States. 3. Child rearing—United States. 4. Work and family—United States. I. Title.
HQ759.L48 1986 640'.43'0880431 85-48125
ISBN 0-689-11556-3

Published simultaneously in Canada by Collier Macmillan Canada, Inc.
Manufactured by Fairfield Graphics, Fairfield, Pennsylvania
Designed by Kathleen Carey
First Edition

THIS BOOK IS DEDICATED TO
ALL WORKING MOTHERS

those who contributed to it
those who read it
those who care for our children
those who try to survive and cope
those who try to enrich their lives

AND

to our daughters for whom, I hope,
the choices will be easier.

ACKNOWLEDGMENTS

First, my love and deepest gratitude to the members of my immediate family, my incomparable network, who have encouraged and actively supported my choices. They have shared a part of their lives with this project since 1979, and I am eternally grateful for their dedication.

My husband, Bob, who believed in independent persons within marriage, equal marital partnership, and participatory daddyhood before even I was aware of their importance, helped me to be the me I am. In 1960, he convinced me to work through my own feelings of guilt and insisted on what experts claim to be true today: if you are happy, your children will be happy! Bob gave me the emotional "space" to work and he physically created my workspace. He supplied my writing tools and assumed many household tasks (or ignored the undone ones) so I could use those tools. He deserves special thanks for giving me everything I ever wanted from him: unlimited love, boundless enthusiasm, and redheaded daughters.

Our daughters, Alison, Sharon, and Jenifer, who blossomed into womanhood while I wrote, accepted my need to be my own person and taught me many of the mothering skills I have acquired. Though different in many ways, they share common attributes. Each is bright, caring, and creative. Moreover, each has discovered for herself, upon leaving home, that she is hard-working, responsible, and totally capable of living on her own.

My parents, Anne and Sol Siegel, who have supported me in every endeavor of my life, particularly as a working mother, are still there for me at a time when many daughters are caring for parents.

Second, I want to thank all the working mothers who willingly gave me their single most precious commodity: time. I am grateful to Sharon Lauer, who opened her address book and shared the names in her extensive network; to the role models, who opened the doors to their offices and homes and contributed their techniques and private feelings, to Millie Guaneri, who typed, gratis, the first chapter in the summer of 1979 so I could get it out before school reopened; to Carol Taurone who typed and retyped, ad infinitum, the entire manuscript and patiently listened to my tales of trying to get published, and to Connie Schwadron, who contributed the information about Social Security Services. My friend Bob Coleman and his associate Andy Rosen, of the accounting firm of Margolin, Winer & Evens, contributed their expertise to help me write the section on tax credits accurately and clearly. I offer thanks and love to those friends and associates who sincerely cared about seeing my "baby" published.

Barbara Kouts, my agent, believed in the book, and her "stick-to-itiveness" brought it to Atheneum. Ann Rittenberg, Associate Editor at Atheneum, gave careful and enthusiastic attention to the manuscript. And, finally, thanks to Susan Leon, my editor at Atheneum, whose new life as the working mother of Joshua has just begun. Thank you for your keen intelligence, clear thinking, and eye for detail. I had faith that an editor would see the value in this book. I didn't know that the person would become so dear to me.

SPECIAL ACKNOWLEDGMENT

Maida G. Berenblatt

I want to pay special tribute to Maida G. Berenblatt, who is the embodiment of the philosophy of this book. She gave me the idea to write a book sharing what we had learned and experienced in hope of easing the lives of other working mothers.

Her significant talents contributed to the structure and format, and she provided the Guilt/Anger Self-Evaluation Workbook. Further, her insights, training, and experience in psychotherapy focused the responses to my questions and helped me to clarify emerging ideas.

In our long-term relationship, as college friends, colleagues, and each other's "working mother network," she has taught me much that I have now shared with you.

Thanks, Maida.

Contents

Do You Do It All?

Give yourself 2 points for each question to which you can answer "yes," 1 point for each "sometimes," and 0 points for each "no."

Yes	*Sometimes*	*No*	
___	___	___	1. Do you do the laundry for everyone in your household, even though each person is capable of riding a bike, driving a car, or controlling other complicated machines—like the television set?
___	___	___	2. Are you in charge of what other family members eat, even when you aren't home to have the meal with them?
___	___	___	3. Does your stomach tighten every time someone asks you a question beginning "How come . . ." or "Why don't you . . ."?
___	___	___	4. Do you find that your time in the office or other workplace is the calmest of your day?
___	___	___	5. Do you worry about "getting it together"?
___	___	___	6. Do you have reservations about being a "real mother"?
___	___	___	7. Do you feel that if it weren't for you, your domestic scene would fall apart?
___	___	___	8. Do you feel that you have no free time for privacy or leisure activities?
___	___	___	9. Are you convinced that if you don't do it all it won't get done?
___	___	___	10. Do the other people in your household cooperate grudgingly or refuse to do their fair share of the household tasks?

SCORE:

0–6 Congratulations—you've got it together! But please read on to pick up some new hints that will make your life even smoother.

7–15 You're juggling everything in your life! As one ball drops you just maintain your balance and manage to scoop it up when another ball falls to the floor. This book will help you keep those balls flowing.

16–20 This book will teach you that although you *can't* do it all, you can still make sure that it all gets done, and knowing this will help you feel better about yourself. Only then can you be at peace with the two major (and apparently conflicting) roles in your life: mothering and working.

Dear Reader,

You've been the "happy homemaker" for years and now you want to go back to work and accomplish something on your own. Or you've been a wage-earning mother from the start and you need more time to feel free and unfettered. Perhaps you spent time building a career before having your first baby, and though it's wonderful to be a mother at last, it's hard to cope after all those years when it was just you and your husband and your two incomes. No matter which way you did it, you explored the choices—marriage? career? children?—and decided to take all three. And whoever you are, the chances are you are one of the thousands of women who are trying to juggle the management of both a personal and professional life.

This book offers a wide range of sane, practical ideas for you, the mother who works, because experience has shown that no matter how hard you try, *you can't do it all*!

In fact, if you want both your personal and professional lives to be as stress-free and happy as possible, you shouldn't even try to do it all. Sure, it all has to get done. But can't a good part of it be delegated or shared? Can't some of it even be eliminated? If your answer is an immediate and resounding "No! Maybe in someone else's house, but not mine!" then read on—this book will show you that it can be done, and it will show you how.

The women who are described on the following pages are family women whose loved ones form a precious part of their lives. Married or single, they have the major responsibility for the day-to-day management of their children's well-being. Most of them offer techniques to help cope with the combined demands of family and career. Some still try to do every single thing the traditional stay-at-home mother does.

All are aware that 100 percent devotion to career would

bring greater success at work, but they, like you, want more than that. They want the warmth of loving relationships in addition to the satisfaction of professional accomplishment. Yet none of them would dream of choosing one way of life over the other.

The choice of the woman who decides to make motherhood her full-time career is no less important than that of one who tries to do both. But no single job presents the problems faced by the mother trying to perform in two full-time careers. It is the purpose of this book to meet the needs of those mothers whose work, at home and in the marketplace, creates conflicts that need to be resolved.

Today the results of these conflicts are more and more in the public eye. Headlines announce:

WOMEN HEAR THAT SUCCESS IS COSTLY

AS WOMEN'S ROLES GROW MORE LIKE MEN'S SO DO THEIR PROBLEMS

WOMEN AND PILLS

A Rand Corporation study on "the dark side of female emancipation" reported that "working wives . . . face role conflicts. They encounter stresses from both work and their husbands to play those [different] roles right."

Working mothers don't need a study to tell them what they already know. When they add the role of mother to their others, they feel additional stress—and a great deal of guilt.

It is a dilemma. As more women each year join the work force, only to rush home and do their housework, the business of life becomes more complex. What do they do about child care? How do they manage their households? Can they fit in the "other people"? Do they have enough leisure time? How do they manage money? And most pressing of all, *how do they handle the guilt?*

It is a standing joke that if you scratch the surface of any working mother you'll find guilt. The problem is that dealing with it just isn't funny!

Television programs and magazine and newspaper articles constantly alert us to the statistical evidence of the danger of stress in the lives of career women with families.

Does all this mean we march back to the kitchen? Of course it doesn't! It means we learn to *reduce our stress* as much as possible.

This book does not offer any pat answers to the problems discussed. Rather, it illustrates the intelligent choices women have made. The women you will meet in this book have been chosen because they have confronted the problems, dealt with the conflicts, and through trial and error have gained confidence in their lives. These women were selected to illustrate particular lifestyles and their individual coping techniques. Whether or not you agree with each woman's choice, you will be able to learn from the way she carried it out.

Let me tell you more about these women. Although they chose employment for various reasons, coming as they do from diverse social, educational, economic, and ethnic backgrounds, their jobs offer them some degree of the following:

- A sense of self
- Financial independence
- Personal satisfaction
- Power
- Challenge
- Approval
- Security
- Achievement
- Recognition
- Respect

In most instances, the women chosen have used admirable skill in determining their choices and acting upon them. The cases of some women have been included to illustrate that sometimes we create our own stressful situations: often, we can recognize what we do only by seeing others doing it.

Most important, as you read about others with whom you will empathize you will gain a greater understanding of yourself. Gathering insight and information will be helpful in your effort to combine your work with motherhood, household management, and love relationships. So read on and discover how your future everyday life can become easier. If you can arrange your household better before starting a new job or having a new baby, your daily stress will be reduced from the very beginning. Once you believe that YOU CAN'T DO IT ALL, it will become easier to adopt some of the new techniques and alternatives suggested in this book.

YOU CAN'T DO IT ALL

THE CHILD CARE CHALLENGE

HOUSEWORK can be postponed. Dinner can be bought at Burger King. Errands can be delegated. Lovers can be stalled. But babies *need* to be changed and fondled. Toddlers *need* devotion, attention, and affection. Sick children *need* to be cuddled and nurtured. School-age children *need* supervision and transportation.

And *you* need to work.

What do you do? From infancy to maturation, children need someone to be there to tend, to transport, and, especially, in the early teen years, to tail along to watch and support their activities. These needs affect all employed parents whose schedules are inflexible. And because most jobs demand time away from home and children, either you must decide upon a career that allows you to determine your own time and place for working or you will need to arrange the best possible child care.

But first you absolutely *must* be able to answer "yes" to this one question:

"Am I willing to share the care for my child with another person?"

Whether you say "yes" with a modified, "If my husband/-

mother/friend babysits" or "yes" with a reluctant, "If I can find the right person" or "If I can afford the help" or "yes" with a confident, "That's the best way to mother" isn't important because, for all of us who chorus "yes," child care is the answer! Once you say "yes," you are ready to explore the situation, consider the options, decide on the alternative that is best for your personal lifestyle, and be at peace with yourself and your decision.

If you cannot say "yes" because you know that you will not be happy to leave your child in anyone else's care, then I think you should seek opportunities that are compatible with that decision.

Contrary to the prevailing doubts of anxious mothers, child care is neither the career obstacle nor the detriment to children that many fear it to be. Rather than child care itself, your perception of child care is what provokes anxiety. Your children are not upset because you work but because they receive the negative vibrations of your guilt about leaving them. All recent studies agree that children of working mothers prosper as fully as children whose mothers stay home with them. The key factor in all cases is the mother: if she feels good about what she does, her children will, too!

For example, you may be perfectly willing to leave your child in the care of its father or grandparents but totally unwilling to leave your child in a day care facility. If that's the case, then you should find a career that matches the time availability of your preferred caregivers. Work evenings, or weekends, or at home, or create a job-sharing opportunity for yourself.

You might, however, have an available grandparent who is willing, even anxious, to tend your child but who you absolutely reject for the job. You might decide that a carefully selected group care facility, in which your child can play with others under trained supervision, is a better answer to your needs.

You may have a trusted friend, who, while at home caring for her own children, offers to watch yours for a small sum of money. Perhaps you refuse to consider this option because you prefer to choose a newcomer who will come to your home to care for your precious child in his/her own familiar surroundings.

Which child care choice you make depends on your own personal attitudes and limitations. Yet once you have decided on the child care method you feel most comfortable with, you will find that you will be freer to enjoy a less stressful life.

A *New York Times* article called "Psychology Is Revising Its View of Women" quotes Dr. Grace Baruch and Dr. Rosalind Barnett, authors of a study on women's lifelong course of development they conducted at Wellesley College, as follows: "The greatest sense of well-being . . . is among women who have high-level jobs, are mothers and are married. Juggling these roles does not stress women. Work seems to be a buffer against the stresses of motherhood because it offers a sense of mastery of a sort that raising children does not." This report by prominent female psychologists shows insights that agree with the feelings expressed by the hundreds of working mothers with whom I've been in contact. They've found a variety of satisfactory child care arrangements. They've expressed a satisfaction they didn't think they'd have if they hadn't combined the two roles. None regretted working while raising their children, and most concluded that their children were better off because they worked. And indeed, most studies agree that children suffer no harm from being tended by mother-substitutes. In fact, many claim they thrive on the extra attention.

I share the confidence of other wage-earning mothers who feel that loving child care contributes not only to the child's well-being but to their own. Having another person with whom to share the delights, concerns, and anxieties, not to mention the aggravations, is most satisfying. In two-parent families, it is a bonus. For single parents, a mother-substitute provides emotional support that is often not available from any other source.

Naturally, because most of the child care solutions are private arrangements, they cost money. This should not be considered a deterrent to the woman yearning to launch a career. Most mothers feel the pinch of paying a salary out of their income. You might very well share your take-home pay equally with the mother-substitute who makes it possible for you to earn your own salary. Many wage-earning mothers do just this and find that the world of work, even at the financial break-even point, is worth every sacrifice.

Because inflation has made life more difficult for growing families and especially for people living on fixed incomes, other mothers, particularly those whose children are grown, are looking for ways to supplement their incomes and may well be available to help care for your child. Here are some other reasons why they are ideal candidates for the job:

- They enjoy caring for children.
- They need to feel appreciated for doing what they do best.
- They often prefer to earn cash.
- They like making independent decisions.
- They prefer not to commute.
- They might not have the marketable skills needed to obtain other employment.
- They might have the skills but not the motivation to join the nine-to-five work force, the dressers for success, or the seasoned commuters.

To illustrate the investment in career that child care represents, let me tell you my own story.

When I got my first paid teaching position in 1959, I brought home $70 every two weeks and handed it over to the housekeeper. In those days, I was lucky to find a person who loved tending our baby and who willingly cared for the house, did laundry, made breakfast, and cleaned up after dinner.

I was in heaven! I came home from work (teaching is demanding but the hours are good for mothering) and spent quality time playing with the baby. People thought I was foolish: "You'll pay more in taxes!" (But I had medical coverage!) "You'll have to buy clothes!" (I couldn't wait!) "It'll cost so much in food!" (But I lingered over coffee and didn't do the dishes!) Needless to say, I was happier working and rushing home to uninterrupted play with my first child.

Although I didn't realize it at the time, nor did those who

thought me a fiscal fool, I was making an investment in my financial future:

- Earnings rise and child care expenses decline with time.
- Benefits accrue (consider medical benefits, pension plans, and matching savings plans).
- Job security offers financial security.

I found that going to work when the children were young ensured my job security. Friends of mine who stayed at home while they raised their children were unable to find teaching positions or were excessed after working a year or two, because they had accrued too few years seniority.

So, when you think about the economics of a career, consider the larger picture. Think down the road five or ten years and project your earnings and child care costs. I'm sure you'll find that child care costs decline from half (or more) of your pay to one-fifth (or less). Here is another way to look at it: parents who pay for child care, followed by nursery school, followed by baby-sitters, don't flinch when the children go to college because they've become accustomed to making room in the budget for such expenses.

If you have great difficulty paying for child care, consider all the low-cost alternatives, including barter arrangements and public day care facilities. From an economic point of view, the low-income person is infinitely better off, financially, while working. This is true even if the struggle is great. Countless mothers have made it, and so will you!

ROLE MODELS

Children First: FRAN

Fran is typical of the woman whose priority is clearly defined. Her family comes first. Fran is a middle-aged woman whose husband's law practice has always provided her with complete financial security. She knows she would have been happier had he chosen to spend more time at home with the family and less time as a workaholic, but she has always accepted the situation. In fact, she is so used to making all the household decisions that she frankly admits she would resent it if he ever expressed enough interest to question her management.

Fran always chose to be there for her children. They were her major priority: "Long after they needed me, I was there to take them, and pick them up, at the school yard."

Fran is the executive director of a statewide volunteer organization. Thousands of people work under her leadership and direction. She controls the organization's lobbying and legislative efforts, and she is its contact and communications person. This is the perfect job for a woman who desires a feeling of achievement and for whom salary is irrelevant, because such positions typically are underpaid. Volunteer organizations cannot afford to pay the salaries the jobs warrant, so the boards of directors are often willing to negotiate and be more flexible with time than are employers who pay top dollar. And it was time, not money, that interested Fran.

From the first, she stipulated her working hours at the office. Although she often worked forty extra hours at home, she was *there*. Remember that money was never an obstacle for Fran. At any time, she had the option to pay for any mother-substitute she needed. But Fran didn't *want* a substitute; she wanted to do the mothering job herself.

For the many years that Fran arranged her work schedule so that she could be home in time for her children, her son, Jonathan, assumed she had spent the whole day at home. Fran never talked about her job. Thus, it never interfered with their needs. She laughed when she admitted that her son Jonathan was almost fourteen before he realized that his mother had another interest that took up some of her time.

Her career offers her a sense of self, a feeling of achievement, importance, and power. She has always done excellent work and been recognized for her efforts. Yet she has always managed to be there for her children and for her husband, too. It's not a bad life, even though it requires hard work and intense organization.

Fran's Solution: Be There

Fran's priority was to be there for her children, but since she needed the challenge and stimulation of work outside her home, she arranged a career according to her family's schedule. One must recognize that Fran was able to acquire a job that allowed her to be flexible about time and to bring work home. These advantages are not always available to women who need their income to pay for basic needs.

Fran's decision is valid for her. It works for thousands of women who combine their commitments to their children with a full-time, part-time, and flexible job schedules. But a situation that is ideal for a woman like Fran is totally unavailable for many women who are dependent on their incomes. Let's read about the decision of a woman who doesn't enjoy Fran's economic freedom.

Support System First: SHERRY

Sherry is a dynamic, self-starting individual. Years ago she did volunteer work for a state politician. Today, having skipped over low-paying jobs, she has parlayed her volunteer experience into a successful career that combines financial reward with recognition and some power.

When we first met, she felt stifled in a marriage in which her role was simply to be there as a supportive spouse. As the wife of an entrepreneur, she was expected to serve the coffee, feed the business guests, accompany him when he wished, and be the "good woman." She never thought it was terrible; it was just not what she wanted after ten yers of married life.

Sherry left her comfortable, traditional lifestyle when they were divorced. For the next few years she had to cope with no child support, no alimony, and the total responsibility of caring for their child. Like many single mothers, she spent much of her time and energy, in the beginning, in court trying to collect child support.

Sherry channeled the anger she felt to constructive purposes. With her daughter at her side, she became a feminist activist. Her struggle for financial independence began. She campaigned for human rights issues and gained positive recognition. Soon she was rewarded with her first paid position. She then used her contacts and her energies to create new and better positions for herself.

By renting a room in her apartment to graduate students, Sherry helped pay her rent and at the same time acquired a child care support system. She bartered fifteen hours a week for a rent reduction. Although the students did not do any housekeeping, someone was there in the evenings when Sherry was at meetings. This provided a sense of security and positive role models for her child, who was at school while her mother was at work. The student paid low rent for a nice room in an apartment in a city where dwellings were both hard to find and expensive.

Today, years later, child care is less of a problem. Sherry still has a renter sharing the apartment because her work requires some travel and her child needs company. After-school sitters often accompany and pick up the child to after-school activities.

Because the child's father has not played an active role in her upbringing since the divorce, and Sherry felt her own survival was the key to her success, both as a person and as a mother, her choice was "survival first." If she was not economically self-sufficient, her child's well-being was in jeopardy.

A paid, full-time sleep-in mother-substitute would have been perfect. But as any struggling person knows, the best is not always affordable. Sherry's choice worked for her and for her daughter.

Would it work for you?

Sherry's Solution: Rent a Room

For someone like Sherry, with space but little money, letting a room is an option. In large cities, where rents are high and rooms almost unavailable, this arangement is commonplace. In college towns it is a way of life. Students and senior citizens who live in can sometimes care for children or exchange services as a part of their rent.

Whether you pay the live-in help or they pay you, these arrangements must be well defined and the person chosen must be carefully screened. The "other" person may become more of a headache than a benefit, as, for example, if his or her problems become the problems of your family. Some people complain that college students are more of a nuisance than the toddler they are supposed to care for.

But often these arrangements make good sense and provide your children with another person with whom to relate, or rely upon, when you cannot be there. Naturally, it is important to interview* any and all mother-substitutes as carefully as possible and to check personal references.

When our third daughter was born, our family was lucky enough to hire an au pair who had spent a year working nearby. She agreed to work for us provided she was free to go out at night after her obligations at home were completed. (Formerly she had been allowed only one night off a week.) I agreed providing she would promise to be awake and alert in the morning.

After completing these negotiations, our family spent years with someone we all cherished. It was wonderful to have her help make breakfast, tend to the children, and baby-sit whenever we wanted to go out. Some of my friends and acquaintances have been lucky enough to live with the same housekeeper for ten or fifteen years or more and feel the security of knowing that their children (as well as their homes) are watched over by a caring and responsible individual.

All the obstacles live-in help may involve seem to vanish when you find the right person for your family. The lengthy search then becomes worthwhile, and the expense becomes worth the price tag. My advice if you plan to hire live-in help is succinct: if you find the right person, be generous, kind, considerate, and willing to negotiate.

Survival First: KIM

Kim has good reason to feel satisfied. She supports her daughter. She pays her bills. She enjoys, and is appreciated, at work. She has a future to look forward to with confidence. But only

*See "Interviewing a Mother-Substitute," page 45.

a few years ago Kim illustrated the plight of countless single mothers who marry young, give birth to babies before twenty and find themselves alone with responsibilities too large to handle independently. Like others, Kim survived by virtue of her own hard work supplemented, temporarily, by support services provided by the Department of Social Services.

I met Kim when she was a student in my Spanish class during her ninth grade year. Sweet natured, bright, and diligent, at fourteen, she displayed two qualities I admire: a sense of responsibility and a willingness to work for what she wanted.

Later, in her senior year, Kim worked as an office aide and we continued our relationship in brief, but intimate, conversations. She talked about her boyfriend. I talked about scholarship opportunities. She talked about "getting married". I talked about marriage. When she lifted her hand she showed me a tiny diamond stone instead of a class ring. She talked about the wedding. I talked about birth control and the advantages of education and the ability to earn one's own living. She replied "Oh, I don't have to worry about that. My fiancé has a good job. Besides, he doesn't want me to go to school or work after we get married."

I stopped talking and wondered why she continued to seek my friendship.

Two years later she stopped by for a visit—with her baby daughter. She was dressed entirely in pink, with enormous dark eyes like her mommy's and a smile that never stopped. Everything was fine.

The next time they appeared it was obvious that Kim's world had collapsed. Her husband had disappeared the month before and Kim had heard that he'd left the country. Her own sad eyes said it all: Where to? What next?

That day when we talked Kim listened. Her alternatives were slim and we knew it. Kim acted almost immediately.

She applied for Social Services and discovered that she could get support and Day Care for her child while she enrolled in a two year course leading to a specific occupational goal. Kim enrolled in a local community college where she earned straight A's. Her child was tended in a neighborhood group care home where one Day Care mother cared for her own child and five others.

When my classroom phone announced a visitor and Kim appeared I saw a new woman. Confidently and proudly she showed her Associate's Degree and beautiful letters of recommendation from her teachers. Soon thereafter she found employment as a secretary. Kim's financial independence is a result of her hard work and services provided for women in her position. Day Care is the core of those services and helps single mothers and their children survive.

Kim's Solution: Day Care

Like Kim, many single parents find themselves without alimony, child support, a job to support the family, or a family member available to watch the children. So, if you are a woman to whom success is synonymous with self-sufficiency and whose major obstacle is the lack of money to pay the sitter, this information is for you!

This book is meant to serve as a road map to help readers reach a destination with maximum efficiency and minimum stress. I hope to point out the pitfalls and roadblocks along the way, to offer alternative routes, and to help you reach your goal.

The major roadblock for parents of young children is the difficulty in finding adequate day care. Naturally, this obstacle increases in inverse proportion to the amount of money you have available. Therefore, this section is especially geared to mothers whose financial resources are minimal.

Many women have felt overwhelmed by this situation. They have sought aid, applied for loans, and received public assistance. Some have taken advantage of every educational benefit they could find, located adequate day care facilities for their children, and become self-supporting within five years.

So, whether you need public assistance or can sustain yourself without it, let's look at the situation from one point of view: How can you get the best care for your children at the least financial cost?

Don't overlook the day care facilities that might be available in your community sponsored by religious institutions, civic associations, colleges, business, or industrial firms. The day care

A BASIC PRIMER OF SOCIAL SERVICES RELATIVE TO DAY CARE

1. *AFDC,* Aid to Families with Dependent Children: Social Services offers assistance to financially qualified families in which one parent is either absent or disabled. Funds are allocated as follows: 50 percent federal; 25 percent state; 25 percent county.
2. *HR:* Home Relief is public assistance offered to any family in need of supplementary income. Funds are allocated as follows: 50 percent state; 50 percent county.
3. *CASSPP;* Comprehensive Annual Social Services Program Plan. Services include estimating the number of children needing day care, and the proposing of day care centers and day care homes (up to six children for each home).
4. *Title XX Federal Social Security Act:* This law controls the funds used to pay for day care. Although you might assume that only parents on public assistance are entitled to enroll their children in public day care facilities, slots are available for families not receiving public assistance.
5. *Slots:* A slot is the space made available for each child. Naturally, the budget determines how many slots are available, which means how many children can be cared for. The agency has to determine whether you qualify according to a "needs assessment."
6. *Needs assessment:* This is the department's method of determining whether your family is eligible for the public assistance facility. When you go to the Depart-

ment of Social Services you can go to the Public Assistance Office and say, "I want to apply for public assistance" (money), or, you can go to Day Care Services only and say, "I wish to apply to see if my child(ren) are eligible for public day care."

7. *Mandated/nonmandated services:* CASSPP offers services mandated according to the requirements of Title XX. In addition to the mandated services which include day care (those required by federal statute), some local districts offer other services. Each level of government must follow federal guidelines but can add services according to the community's priorities. The nonmandated service of your town, city, or county might provide what you need, such as counseling or referrals.
8. *Income eligibility standards:* This refers to the method of calculating eligibility. In New York State (and it differs from state to state), the median income of a family of four is used as the standard. If your family earns a certain percentage of the median income (based on the number of people in the family), you are eligible. If you know that you meet the federal poverty standards, your child probably qualifies for day care.
9. *Lien guaranteeing penny-for-penny payment for services rendered:* A lien entitles the Department of Social Services to get payment back from you when you sell the item on which a lien is placed. For example, if you own a house, the Department of Social Services requires you to sign a lien so it will be paid back when or if that property is sold. The penny-for-penny requirement, however, appears to differ from county to county even within a state. For instance, in Suffolk County, New York, my research indicates that the penny-for-penny lien applies to 100 percent of aid granted but excludes day care (services only). In Nassau County, this lien is discretionary and rarely implemented. It is important to investigate all facts if you need or qualify for day care.

available does not begin to meet the need, but aggressive searching might uncover just what you require. Mothers have a way of creating their own community day care in apartment buildings or suburban neighborhoods. If you seek out community organizations and women's centers you'll meet women who have done it and who might lead you to the right place.

If you feel that you might be eligible for a government-supported day care facility gather the information necessary to find out whether you qualify. Children from families who do not receive public assistance are sometimes eligible for certain services offered by the Department of Social Services, including day care. Therefore, it is important to gain a basic understanding of the system.

Call your local Department of Social Services for complete and accurate information.

Since out-of-home child day care is available only as a necessary part of a plan for self-support, it is important to be aware that you will have to be employed, or participating in an *approved* program of vocational training, or be involved in education leading to a specific occupational goal.

This information may lead you to a logical detour. If you find your skills can't get you the job you need to survive on a long-term basis, and you feel you can sustain yourself for a short time while attending school, try to obtain financial aid for your education. With financial aid, loans, and the day care available on campus, you might find that this detour is the most direct route to self-sufficiency.

Career First: PHYLLIS

Eighteen years ago, it was still somewhat unusual for young women of twenty to put their careers ahead of marriage or family. Phyllis was one of those who did. She was always ambitious, and in school she was an "achiever." Her goals were crystal clear, perhaps because she was the daughter of professional parents. Phyllis graduated from college without the mandatory diamond on her finger and entered law school the following fall. Her goals were established, and she was ready to achieve them.

Don't think she didn't hear about wedding bells and baby carriages. After all, even professional mothers in the late 1960s worried when their twenty-three-year-old daughters were on the verge of becoming "old maids." Sons got their share of the guilt trips when they chose to remain free until thirty, but daughters were very much expected to marry and produce a grandchild or two. Living together (heaven forbid) was not yet discussed, and marrying out of the religion, though unacceptable, was better than not marrying at all.

Work had its share of problems, too. Women lawyers used to have unmentionable reputations, and in the corporate office that hired Phyllis, she had to work double time to prove she was both a competent attorney and a nonthreatening person.

Because she chose to devote herself to her work, Phyllis found dating difficult. Phyllis was not the only woman I interviewed who mentioned the double standard that still exists concerning working late at the office. It is still acceptable for a man to cancel, postpone, or otherwise delay a social appointment because he has to work late, but even in the 1980s, it is less acceptable for working women to do so. Phyllis found that dates disappeared after the second time she postponed or canceled an engagement to work late at the office.

In spite of the career obstacles that existed in the 1960s, Phyllis earned a remarkable reputation and settled into the comfortable, if somewhat lonely, life of the successful professional. At thirty, she decorated her own apartment. It was a difficult time for her. Never feeling as though she had to wait for a man to come along, she chose her possessions carefully, planning for a future life alone. She came to grips with the medical beliefs that existed then and accepted having motherhood pass her by.

Perhaps because she had settled into a life of career satisfaction supplemented by the comfort of dear friendships, Phyllis relaxed and began to enjoy her thirties as an independent woman. She looked around her and saw a revolution among women who had made different choices and found that they were seeking what she had. Within a year, she met and married Paul. Within the next two years, Phyllis gave birth to two babies.

Phyllis's story is typical of the thousands of women who chose to have their first child when they were between the ages of thirty and forty. If you are familiar with the birth statistics today, you will realize that the birth rate is rising among only two age groups. Very young girls (under sixteen) are having more babies, and so are women over thirty. Although these adult women chose motherhood in spite of medical warnings and widespread fears, they are proof that the wait was worthwhile.

There is a lot to be said for waiting before one starts a family. The advantage of maturity certainly offsets the slight loss in energy and vitality. Moreover, men and women who wait until they are past thirty rarely resent staying in or undertaking familial responsibilities.

From an economic point of view, having children later is much simpler. People over thirty usually have more financial security than those I call "child parents." Every pair of shoes and each dental visit is a crisis for people who are young and/or poor. Mortgage payments and telephone bills are overwhelming responsibilities. People who plan and postpone their parenting tend to have their financial affairs in better control than those to whom children "happened" when they were younger.

For the working mother who chose "career first" before starting a family, waiting has all kinds of rewards. She never wonders what might have been, if only. . . . She can usually afford the best possible housekeeper or mother-substitute to care for her children. More important, with her career well established she can often afford to make changes in her time schedule if she chooses.

Phyllis did just that. Although she worked until just before the births of her children, taking six weeks off the first time and a month the second, she did make changes in her career to allow more family time.

Both Phyllis and Paul work five days a week. On Friday evenings, briefcases bulging, suitcases stuffed, they leisurely drive to their house on the eastern end of Long Island. Once a bachelor's pad for summer sun, it now houses a warm, loving family for year-round rest and relaxation. Without the sitter/housekeeper to infringe on privacy, Phyllis and Paul take turns with the cooking and child care; occasionally they hire a teenaged sitter and go out for an evening together.

Although the children haven't started school yet, Phyllis mentioned that she and her husband were thinking about changing their schedules when that time comes. Perhaps they'll leave Friday at three, perhaps they'll each take a work break once a week to be there after school. Whatever solution they choose, they will plan it equitably.

Like two people given gifts they never expected to get, Phyllis and Paul enjoy their family and careers together. With two incomes and shared parenting, they leave no doubt that "career first" can be an idyllic arrangement.

Phyllis's Solution: Sleep-in Housekeeper

For many families, particularly those with adequate space and money, the ideal solution to the child care problem is live-in help. For families with small children who rise early or who need nighttime attention, or for parents whose work schedules are erratic or involve travel, live-in help might be the only practical solution.

For the mother to whom survival is a priority, it is difficult to comprehend the many problems that arise in finding someone who can live with the family and tend to the children. I spent years hiring the least expensive household workers because that was all I could afford. I experienced having to tend young women, far from home, who were fearful and unhappy. One came directly from the agency and went to her room to unpack, only to emerge drunk an hour later. Naturally, by that time the agency was closed!

My two-year-old (she's now past twenty-five) used to make

life difficult for the helpers she didn't like. Once, after smearing toothpaste all over the tub, she said, "But I was nice to Kathy!" I realized then that even toddlers know best who cares about them and who doesn't. I learned to trust the judgment of my child as well as my own.

WHAT TO REMEMBER WHEN HIRING SLEEP-IN HOUSEKEEPERS

1. *Do expect it to cost more.* Minimum wage multiplied by forty is a fair rule of thumb for a weekly base salary. Add to that a private room with television, food, some transportation expenses, the use of utilities, shampoo, and other sundries. Consider a two-week paid vacation as part of the salary the first year. Do give small frequent raises or bonuses.
2. *Do expect to get what you pay for.* A household worker at the lowest salary often needs to be trained to use the phone or to operate household machines. If you want an experienced person with excellent references, expect to pay for these qualities.
3. *Do expect your household worker to work a five-day week.* Frequently Monday to Friday is the rule with weekends off. Many work a five-and-a-half-day week.
4. *Do expect to make plans in advance* and tip substantially if you expect someone to work overtime.
5. *Do expect to pay an agency fee* unless you are willing to spend a great deal of energy interviewing.
6. *Do think twice about hiring illegal aliens* or bringing someone into the country and guaranteeing a job. The houseworker may be the very best, but the legal complications are difficult.
7. *Do think about language facility* while your children are developing their basic linguistic skills (I'm a language teacher, able to communicate in Spanish and French, but I wanted by children to hear decent English).

8. *Do expect to share the housekeeping* or to hire someone else to do heavy cleaning chores. Just as full-time mothers need help with housework, full-time housekeepers who care for children all day cannot be expected to do all the cleaning.
9. *Do spell out the responsibilities* clearly in advance.
10. *Do consider the total legal responsibility* of employers.

(See also the sections "How to Hire a Mother Substitute," and "Legal Responsibilities to Household Employees," Appendix 2, and "Tax Credit for Child Care Expenses," Appendix 3.)

We All Come First: DOROTHY

Dorothy said it best: "Each one is a priority: my job, my children, my mate, and my future career. We just juggle them all until everything falls into place." Dorothy manages her life with a great deal of skill. You will hear about her again later because she has many techniques worth sharing.

When I first met her, we were only two of the many working mothers who arranged child care coverage and took off days from work to lobby our legislators for the passage of the Equal Rights Amendment. I was immediately impressed by her straightforward professionalism. She had a strong awareness of sensitive issues, total knowledge of the facts, and a manner of presenting them coolly. When I decided to find women to interview for this book, Dorothy was one of the first I invited. When I wrote to her, I knew nothing about her personal status. We met on a frosty winter day, and over a hot cup of soup I asked her about herself. This is what I learned.

Dorothy was a librarian. Like other women whom I interviewed, she was supporting herself at this job while accumulating the necessary credentials for a more lucrative and, she hoped, more rewarding career. She gave me time to speak to her after work but before her evening classes. She was on her way to school to complete the master's degree she needed for a job in labor management.

At home, she has a teenage child from an early and unsuccessful marriage. She is newly remarried, and since I had last seen her she had given birth to a second child. Because she lives in a household with a teenager, a toddler, and a new husband on top of her job and college commitments, I expected to hear all sorts of complications. Instead, I listened to a woman whose act was very together.

Dorothy is the living essence of the philosophy of this book. Her attitude is positive, and she perceives of no problems that can't be solved. When complications develop, the family meets and discusses a solution. She suffers no guilt and bears no great stress.

When I asked Dorothy how she managed her household, she said simply: "With a toddler at home, child care is our most important priority. Obviously, someone must be with her at all times.

"We have a marvelous sitter who watches her during the day, and the three of us [she includes her thirteen-year-old here] sit down every Sunday night and divide the child care coverage for the week. My school schedule, his meetings, and a teen's social life leave each of us evenings to tend to the baby. We have a baby-sitter available, but rarely need her.

"It is my sitter I want to tell you about. She is marvelous." Dorothy's salaried mother-substitute offers the parents complete confidence and no worry. She happens to live in the same high-rise, subsidized, middle-income housing project as Dorothy. So the first piece of good fortune is obvious. Dorothy transports her child to the sitter by elevator. Moreover, her sitter is a true professional, whose attitude and competence alleviate any worry a parent might have. Dorothy has no doubts that she is doing what is best for her child, herself, and the total family.

A former elementary school teacher, Dorothy's salaried mother-substitute tired of both the educational bureaucracy and the stress of teaching large numbers of children. She chose instead to devote her attentions and her abilities to caring for a small number of children in her own home. Knowing that her energy level must be conserved, she never baby-sits evenings or weekends. She guards her strength for the hours when she cares for six little ones.

Because the salaried mother-substitute is concerned with nutrition, Dorothy is assured that her baby is well fed. Healthy snacks and lunch provide adequate nourishment. This sitter is warm, reliable, loving, creative, and happy with her chosen work. For Dorothy's family, she is the solution to the child care challenge. Dorothy has no sense of guilt, which is as much a statement about her togetherness as it is about her choice of a successful mother-substitute.

Dorothy typifies the career woman who is happy with her personal and professional lives. Simplification is her motto, and she manages on a very tight budget without an expensive staff. For some reason it all seems effortless to her.

Dorothy's Solution: Working Mothers Help Working Mothers Work

Dorothy is one of millions of working mothers who bring their children to the home of another working mother whose job is to take care of children. Granted, Dorothy has the uncommon advantage of transporting her child by elevator. But many women find other mothers right in their neighborhood who have chosen to stay at home with their own children and earn money by caring for a few more children. These people often give warm, tender, and loving care to all the children.

This alternative has some major advantages:

- It is usually very economical. The fee is normally lower than that charged by a sitter who comes into your own home because the mother is caring for her own child and perhaps a few others, as well as yours. Moreover, if you need to count pennies, the expense of utilities, food, phone, and so on adds up. In this case. they add to your neighbor's bills, rather than your own.
- The sitter is often a reliable member of the community,

known to many, and therefore easier to trust than a stranger.

- You can interview the sitter at her home and make important observations and decisions there.

There are some disadvantages:

- Transporting your child to a sitter adds time to your work day because you have to dress your child and then take him/her out. At the end of the day, you'll probably have to wait and/or chat.
- Your child(ren) might not get along with the others, and this can cause problems, particularly if the sitter is a friend.
- You will still need a backup sitter for times when your child(ren) or the others are sick.

When you interview a working mother at her house,*

- you will be able to make comments such as "Wow! Your house is immaculate. How will you be able to keep it like this?" (The last person you want, in my opinion, is someone who will ignore your darling(s) while she is polishing the mirrors.)
- You can watch to see whether she smokes cigarettes, if that is important to you.
- You can check the quality of toys and playthings as well as the obvious safety and fire precautions.
- Usually, this working mother has her own child(ren) at home. Discuss fully how she plans to deal with jealousy, tiffs, and other problems among the children. Mention specific situations such as: "How do you think you would handle it if your child kicked mine when playing with a favorite toy?"
- Remember that in someone else's home your child might not be the only person in the limelight. Peer play is wonderful, but a healthy balance of attention is necessary.

Dorothy, along with many other mothers, finds that it works to take her child to a sitter. Frankly, I tried it once and didn't

*See "Interviewing a Mother-Substitute," page 45.

like it. My child missed playing with her friends on the block, and I missed having someone to call to defrost a steak or straighten the kitchen or do the laundry. I have never hired anyone to work for me who didn't willingly do those chores. I also found that the economics were about equal and that the person who would come to our house was as loving and reliable as anyone to be found in the neighborhood.

Education First: AMY

Amy and I have been friends for about fourteen years. When we first met, she had just given birth to her first child and I to my third. We taught together in the same school and, as working mothers everywhere do, chatted a great deal about our families. We created our own little "mother network" at work.

During the span of our relationship, children and child care have been the main topics of conversation, followed by education. At first, we discussed our own education. As time passed, we discussed our children's nursery schools, public schools, and high schools. Coincidentally, we not only taught in the same district, but Amy's family moved to the same neighborhood elementary school my children atended. We continued to discuss teachers, programs, parochial versus private schools, and when our children became ready, public versus private colleges. Yes, education was a part of our relationship.

When Amy first became pregnant, her husband had just gone back to school and she was supporting the family. She planned the first pregnanacy carefully and gave birth in August. She taught until June and returned to teach in September. It worked so well for her that she planned it twice again in two-year intervals. Education was such an important concern that as soon as her husband graduated from college Amy started night school herself and has been accumulating degrees and credentials ever since. Today, she is almost finished with her Ph.D. and administrative courses in the field of education and is a junior high school principal.

From the very beginning, our long conversations often included child care options and our different needs. My children, who were lucky enough to be surrounded by two grandmothers and a multitude of aunts and cousins, preferred young energetic sitters—people who skated with them! They complained that older ones were overprotective—not in those words, but by moaning about little details like "She always makes my hat soooo tight!"

Amy, on the other hand, had no family nearby and made a firm decision that what she wanted for her little ones was a loving, mature adult who would become a part of the family, like a grandmother. So, while I had different but wonderful students or au pairs, Amy put the following ad in the paper:

> Mature adult needed to care for infant, experienced child care, no housework. Own transportation, reliable, loving, references necessary!

Amy hired Mrs. Black. She was a widow with no family responsibilities, and she was chock-full of TLC. She became devoted to each of the babies when they were born and became a part and parcel of the family scene. Moreover, although she never did any cleaning, she always prepared the children's meals, tidied the kitchen, and mended anything in sight. Mrs. Black sewed on buttons and baked cookies. Amy drove the children to lessons and coached Little League.

Amy's Solution: Daily Sitter

There are many advantages to hiring a local person to come to your house each day. The nature of the position usually attracts people, especially adult women, who are stable members of the community. They frequently have spent their lives being needed, and with their own nest emptied they have a sincere desire to take care of children. After all, this was the job they were raised to do, prepared to do, and enjoyed doing. Now, with inflation, the difficulties of being a displaced homemaker, or the problem of living on a fixed income, they need to earn a living, too.

In our society it is looked down upon to be a domestic. The jobs involved are the same ones performed by housewives and mothers all over the world, but the attitude toward doing those jobs as paid help is not one of proper respect. If you omit cleaning chores from the job description, you can find the most wonderful people to sit for your child, and you don't have to dress the child or worry about him/her/them getting undivided attention. Although cleaning the house might not be a part of the sitter's job, more often than not she will be willing to do some light housekeeping tasks if asked in a sensitive manner. When you interview, inquire about the person's willingness to do the children's laundry, for example, or to start a meal for the family.*

Few mothers can afford live-in help, but most have to pay for a sitter. Then, as they achieve some financial freedom, these mothers hire a housecleaning service or a weekly housekeeper to come in to help clean the house.

The best part of all is that this sitter will often be with your children throughout the years they need company and caring. Sitters are often willing to reduce their working hours, or to change them, to suit the needs of your growing family. Like Mrs. Black, who was first hired to tend to infants and then to come after school and stay until bedtime, they become like family members.

This common regard for your children often creates close bonds, and the nature of your relationship might be described as camaraderie. I've even seen an occasion when a single parent had one longtime sitter who left, jealous, when the mother remarried and another person came on the scene. Nevertheless, these close relationships breed great trust. With trust, there is no need for guilt. After all, what could be better than a loving mother? Having a loving mother and a loving mother-substitute, that's what!

*"Interviewing a Mother-Substitute," page 45.

WORKBOOK PAGES STEP BY STEP TO YOUR OWN PERSONAL DECISION

Step One: Establish Priorities

Answer whether each of the following statements is true or false:

1. "Good" mothers have to "be there" for their children. ______
2. No one else can raise my children as well as I can. ______
3. My husband won't *let* me get a job. ______
4. Children don't need to learn responsibility; they will have enough of it when they are older. ______
5. Children need love and attention, but it is less significant from whom they receive it. ______
6. Happy children have parents who are people first. ______
7. I can be both a career woman and a fine mother. ______
8. Helpers come and go; children don't confuse real mothers with substitutes. ______
9. Working parents create healthy, independent offspring. ______

10. I chose to have children, so I must stay home with them. ______
11. Children respect the mother who works. ______
12. Children resent the mother who works. ______
13. It would destroy me to miss an event of importance in my child's life. ______
14. If I don't do it for them, they'll think I don't love them. ______
15. My life is mine, theirs is theirs, and we coexist through cooperation. ______

How Do You Feel

Most studies agree that happy mothers make happy children. The determining factor in whether you are going to be happy working while someone else cares for your child is your feelings. If you are already working, and things aren't going well, perhaps it's because of these feelings.

Answer these three questions with brutal honesty:
1. Can you deal with not being there for your child?
____
____

2. Can you deal with the loss of control sharing children entails? ______________________________
____

3. Can you handle all the financial and emotional responsibilities of working and mothering? ______________________________
____

If you do not have positive feelings about these questions, and you have the choice, perhaps you should spend the next few years gaining credentials and/or experiences to help you reenter the work force at a later date when you feel more comfortable.

Step Two: Consider Alternatives

This chart helps you to distinguish different forms of child care at a glance. For a more complete explanation, see Appendix 1, "Glossary of Child Care Terminology," page 247. The $ signs rank the financial expense: $ = cheapest to $$$$$ = most expensive.

ALTERNATIVES	*ADVANTAGE*	*PRICE TAG*
Child at workplace Workplace at home Rearrange career to suit child care	Meet child's needs No cost	Rarely available Career sacrifice
$$$$$ Nurse-governess	At-home care	No housework Expensive
$$$-$$$$ Live-in housekeeper	Full-time help Convenient Housework	Expensive Loss of privacy Culture gap
$$ Mother-substitute Baby-sitter	Individual attention	Reliability Transportation
$$ Out-of-home Group care home Sitter's home	Peer play Trained caregivers Lower cost No household expense	Divided attention You transport Requires contingency plan
$$ Au pair Mother's Helper	Full-time care Some housework Youth Individual attention Inexpensive	Short term Culture gap Youth Loss of privacy
$ Family Member	Loving care Trustworthy Low cost	Rarely available Conflicts in style Loss of control

Step Three: Is the Price Tag Worth It?

It is relevant, when considering the cost of going to work, to think of more than the financial expenses. Changes beget changes. When you choose to grow in new directions, people close to you might respond to these changes in negative as well as positive ways. Often their personal needs determine how they react to your decision. Before you can begin to accept the consequences of whatever decision you choose to make, it is worthwhile to evaluate the price tag.

Most working mothers experience some of the following costs to varying degrees:

Loss of aproval. Ranking along with guilt, and often provoking it, is loss of the approval of others. This is a difficult problem for working mothers. One should ask, "Am I ready to be satisfied with self-approval even if working costs me some loss of approval from those I love?"

This disapproval may range from the most threatening ("If you want to stay married, you'll stay at home," or "If you really loved me, you'd want to be a *real mommy*") to less overt forms of disapproval.

Disapproval may be expressed in the following ways:

- When you start to talk about work, *they* change the subject to the children.
- When you want to share your excitement about your work, *they* mention the negative effects on the family.
- They tell others they are proud of you, but at home, constantly say things like, "There's nothing to eat around here" (since you-know-what), "Didn't you go to the cleaners *yet*?" (you always used to), or "George's mother was at practice today" (while *you* were working).

Loss of approval seems to be more severe for the person who has the least economic need to work. For the woman supporting her family, work is not a negative factor. She is the *good* woman.

But if you are married to a man who earns the family's living, and you choose to leave your family to work, you might be the subject of severe disapproval. It might range from "Don't you realize you're taking money away from someone who *needs* the job?" to "You are just selfish in pursuing your *personal* interests" to "Most women would feel *lucky* to live your life."

Loss of approval is the first step toward suffering guilt, so consider carefully if you are ready before making the big decision. You can develop the coping skills necessary to deal with loss of approval when you believe strongly that your job at home is not your only raison d'être. Family meetings and frank discussions of your personal needs can help you to cope.

Guilt and other stress symptoms. Reason does not always overshadow the one particular guilt that working mothers share. It is wise to consider that even with the finest mother-substitute, even one who is a trained nurse, working mothers suffer guilt. When mothers are at work and their children are sick at home, good daddies call home but good mommies feel they should be there. You must be realistic in realizing this is a myth still considered fact among many people. Sometimes you cannot be there. Can you cope with that?

Financial burden. It is imperative to figure out the economics of employment on a long-term basis to decide whether the financial rewards of working are worth the effort. This is not a determining decision but one to consider seriously. For some people, work can be an expensive luxury worth the price tag. For most, the investment in child care is financially sound.

Cost of time. Each person must make an individual decision on the value of the time involved in career activities and how it relates to the family.

Cost of physical and emotional energy. Each of us must consider the amount of energy we have and how it should be best spent.

Increase in responsibilities. Working mothers frequently balance the increase in their self-esteem against the increase in their responsibilities. This helps to determine the worth of their work.

Loss of control. Once we make the decision to share the responsibility of caring for our children, we must accept the consequences of that decision.

One of the most serious consequences, and for some mothers it is the determining one, is a partial loss of control over the child. No matter who else cares for your child there will be compromises (or differences in style) in the child's upbringing.

Some parents find differences in child rearing an area of incompatibility. These differences should be discussed fully so that you choose a person to care for your child who will best fit your individual needs.

Step Four: Positive Effects

Benefits for Children

Self-Reliance. This is the key issue! Obviously you will not and cannot be there at all times, but the best gift you can give your children is to help them feel good about themselves. How can this be accomplished? Children have to discover their own magic. They do this by learning they are able. Knowing that your children are well cared for, you can be out creating your own magic, thus giving your children the space to discover *their* own magic, too.

Role models. Enough information is available to establish the veracity of the statement that women who work in meaningful roles other than mothering provide their children with positive role models.

Interdependence. If one accepts the philosophy that dependency is a negative goal in raising children, then introducing other people into the child's life is a positive experience. A positive goal is to create *interdependence* in the parent-child relationship. In this situation, one can fulfill the other's needs, but not to the extent that one cannot function without the other. Not being there at every moment, so long as your child's needs are being met, contributes to interdependence.

Trust. Children learn that Mommy or Daddy cannot always be there at every moment, but they trust them to return. Moreover, they learn to trust other people who help them in their daily lives. Of prime importance, they learn to trust themselves.

Materialistic rewards of work. Children learn early the direct correlation between working for pay and the economic benefits. Whether it be food for the table, new sneakers, or something as luxurious as riding lessons, children learn that they reap the benefits of money brought home.

Benefits for Parents

Materialistic rewards of work. Whether the money you earn is used to feed your children or because you "want the best" for your children, earning money is a major source of feeling good about work.

Sense of self. Many mothers work to maintain their own sense of self. Work provides access to feelings of self-worth, accomplishment, and achievement. I've heard stay-at-home mothers confess that they thought it would be more satisfying than it is. "I gave up a good job to be there and no one appreciates me at home," they say. Many women find employment offers that sense of being appreciated.

Security: "I know I can support us if I must." Being in the work force contributes to the ultimate security: knowing you can support yourself and your children financially.

Satisfaction of striving to reach personal goals. Working mothers express the personal satisfaction of working to reach goals they set for themselves.

Tax credit for child care expenses. An explanation of how parents can receive tax credits can be found in Appendix 3, page 259.

Step Five: Where I Stand

I believe that (choose one)

- being there
- having a sleep-in houseworker
- renting a room
- using day care
- hiring a neighborhood mother
- hiring a daily sitter
- other ____________________

is the best child care decision I can make at this time because of

- financial considerations
- my child-rearing beliefs
- convenience to my job
- convenience to my family
- other ____________________

Step Six: Act

My immediate plan is to ____________________________________
These are the things I must do to implement my plan:
1. ____

2. ____
3. ____
4. ____
5. ____
6. ____
7. ____

Suggestions:

- Call agencies and community organizations.
- Check newspapers, religious groups, and senior citizen centers.
- Find a job.
- Place an ad.
- Interview prospective employees.
- Research community resources.
- Compare earning capacity with cost of help.
- Consider earnings versus costs in five years.
- Discuss issue with important advisers.
- Review this section for more ideas!

Finding and Evaluating Child Care

The advantages of organized day care were disclosed in a *New York Times* article on May 29, 1985: "In terms of social and educational skills, children given day care in their own homes or in another's home lag behind children going to organized day care centers and nursery schools." Alison Clarke-Stewart, professor of social ecology at the University of California reported that "children attending nursery school programs scored consistently higher across the board." Among the abilities tested in the 150 children aged two to four were interaction with their mothers, with strangers, and with peers; confidence, playfulness, and assertiveness; and language abilities and memory span. Another study by Kathleen McCartney of Harvard University suggested that day care centers with experienced directors, a high ratio of staff members to children, and ample opportunity for staff memebers to interact individually with each child were among the factors that contributed to children's development of sociability, language skills, and intelligence.

The experts concur that day care alone will not automatically promote positive development. Children need parental support, stimulation, and good genes, too!

Providing the best child care to suit your individual requirements is a three-part process that includes

- Research
- Recommendations
- Evaluation

If you are looking for child care for the first time, it is a good idea to become familiar with the terminology before you even begin your research (see Glossary of Child Care Terminology, p. 247). There seem to be numerous options, but the combination of your individual priorities, limitations, and requirements will limit your viable alternatives.

1. RESEARCH

Let your fingers do the walking. Use this checklist to do research on *group care*. Remember, many of the people who answer the phone will be working mothers—you are not alone!

____ yellow pages; look under "Day Care," "Nursery," "Child Care"
____ library directories of community agencies
____ advertisements in local newspapers
____ churches and synagogues
____ local elected officials
____ state agencies
____ school counseling office
____ women's groups, camps, private schools
____ national sources: if your local research isn't satisfactory, try calling or writing to these agencies:

National Association of the Education of Young Children
1834 Connecticut Avenue, N.W.
Washington, D.C. 20009

National Association for Child Development and Education
500 12th Street, S.W.
Suite 810
Washington, D.C. 20024

Use this checklist to find a *mother-substitute:*
Leave your name and number for them to research and respond.

- _____ newspaper advertisements; look under "Child Care," "Baby-Sitter," "Domestic," "Household Worker," "Au Pair," "Housekeeper," "Room Exchange," "Companion"
- _____ employment agencies; ask about domestic workers
- _____ religious organizations
- _____ senior citizen centers
- _____ women's organizations
- _____ directory of community agencies (yellow pages or library)
- _____ school placement offices (particularly schools that train nurses, teachers, and paraprofessional workers)
- _____ local state employment agency: place a "position available" notice

You might also consider contacting organizations that find housing for women in transition; someone might consider child care in exchange for room and board.

Place your own advertisement in the local newspaper or post it in your building, at the laundromat, or on the grocery store notice board. A carefully worded, well-defined ad will bring results. Here are some examples:

> TLC + Dependability needed! 2 Toddlers, 8 A.M.–6 P.M., light housework, own transportation, experience and references, call evenings 333-3333.

Live rent-free, TV, own bath, exchange 25 hrs week child care, nonsmoker, references. 333-3333 eves & days.

Working mother seeks mother-substitute to care for children 7–10 after school; my home or yours, Sanford district. 333-3333.

Mother-in-law: Come live with a family that wants you! Our children (boys 6–10) want to come home to baked cookies and a hug. No housework. Visit your family on weekends. 333-3333.

Mother-substitute: Take care of our home and preschool children with the same attention you gave yours. Mon.–Fri. 8–6. Must drive, some housework! References. 333-3333.

Housekeeper needed: our busy household needs you! Please love kids, laundry, and feeding hungry children. References. 333-3333.

Working mother needs help to get children off to school and light housekeeping 6 A.M.–9 A.M. (Other hours available for baby-sitting and/or housekeeping.) References. 333-3333.

Discuss wages, household chores and all details on the phone. (See "Interviewing a Mother-Substitute," page 45, and "Checking References," page 43.)

2. RECOMMENDATIONS

- Ask everyone you know (your friends, your pediatrician, office workers, religious institutions, women's center, local elected officials) for recommendations.
- Mention it to everyone you meet, particularly to working women in offices! (Many are working mothers who will help you.)

3. EVALUATION

In addition to asking all the necessary questions and checking the appropriate data, you will want to visit and actually "feel the vibrations" of the people and the place providing child care.

You should also bring your children along. Your instincts will assess the intangibles upon which your ultimate decision might depend. Is it too clean? too quiet? too rigid? Perhaps there was an attitude that made you feel a little uncomfortable. Be as aware of body language as interviewers are when they interview you.

If you feel comfortable with the person or place, your child will. Likewise, trust your children's instincts. If they withdraw or feel uncomfortable, nothing else matters. You won't be content until they are, so include them in your visits and your conversations, and watch carefully to see how your child deals with the person and place and vice versa. Instinctive feelings are important clues, and children's instincts are more clear than our own because they are unencumbered by intellectual factors.

By now, you know your own and your children's priorities. Shopping around may take a little time, but when the end result is a happy child and a mother comfortable with the child's care and well-being, it's worth it.

Evaluating a Group Care Facility

This is a checklist of the basic questions you should ask when you are looking at a prospective group care facility.

- In addition to making a note of the name, address, and telephone number of the facility, ask if there is an after-hours phone at which the director or designated staff memeber can be reached.
- Is the facility convenient to home? to work?
- What are its hours? Are they flexible?
- Is it open during the summer? for half days? before or after school? on weekends? in the evening? during holidays?
- What is its affiliation? Does it offer any special programs?
- What type of child care does it offer? infant care?
- How many children are enrolled in the program? how large is the staff?
- What are the ages of the children? Are there naps? snacks? meals?

- Is there a playground or fenced outdoor space? a playroom? What activities are offered? Are trips scheduled?
- Does the facility have its own transportation?
- Is the facility adequate to my child(ren)'s needs? Is it dirty? too clean?
- Does the staff appear caring? rigid? warm? sexist? impatient? energetic? Do they give the children busywork to keep them quiet? Or do they work and play together?
- What is the tuition? When is it due? Is there a discount for a second child? Any extra charges? Is a portion of the tuition a deductible expense as a charitable contribution?

Interviewing at Any Group Care Facility

Add some of these questions to your own concerns when you are talking with the director of a group care facility or at the home of a group caregiver.

- How do you describe your own and your program's philosophy?
- What is the attitude toward discipline?
- How do you handle all the "what if's"?
  What if my child hit another?
  What if my child cried for a long time?
  What if my child is sick?
- Are you licensed? (What standards do you meet?)
  What must you do to get the license?
  What safety precautions do you take?
- Are unannounced parental visits welcome?
  (It is important to be able to drop in unannounced. Directors might suggest that it disrupts the children, but your children have become [or will soon become] used to your arrival and departure.)
- Can you tell me about the credentials and training of the staff?
  What training is necessary?
  How many staff members were educated to work with children?

What are your criteria for hiring staff members?

- How do you check the moral and ethical character of staff members?
  Do you check references? Criminal records?
  In addition to the teaching staff, who else works in the facility? How are they screened?
- Does your staff meet to discuss programs, children, and problems? How often?
- What are my responsibilities vis-à-vis your program?
- Would you give me the names of three parents whose children are in your program with whom I could discuss it further?

Checking References

Nothing is more important than finding trustworthy help, yet many of us feel embarrassed or apologetic about asking questions to get adequate reference information.

People recommend asking for three references, but I'd add a few more if possible. They need not be work references. People who seek positions caring for children frequently have no prior work experience. Most of them are stay-at-home mothers who enjoyed raising their own children and now need or want to get paid for loving your kids. What is important is not the work experience but the qualities the individual possesses. Your concerns are trustworthiness, reliability, caring, and common sense. These are qualities that any associate can describe. Former teachers, guidance counselors, friends, and personal associates in organizations will be perfectly capable of telling you much that you need to know.

When you ask questions, remember that the idea is to elicit a fairly lengthy response. That way, any fine qualities or liabilities are more likely to come up in conversation. Yes or no answers don't give you much information.

Keep a pencil and notebook handy and keep your notes from various sources together. If you hear the same words again and again, try to read between the lines carefully!

SCRIPT FOR CHECKING REFERENCES

"Hello. Mr./Ms. X gave me your name as a reference. When would be a convenient time for you to answer a few questions?"

"I'm primarily interested in how well Ms./Mr. X deals with children. Could you describe how he/she treated your children? What did they do together?"

"I'm concerned about reliability and dependability. Could you describe Ms./Mr. X in that regard?"

"Could you describe your working relationship/friendship?"

"Is there anything you feel I should know about him/her?"

"I really want this to work out, and you have experience dealing with this person. Is there any advice you could give me to get along well with him/her?"

"Is there anything about this person that you consider a liability?"

"What is the most special asset this person has?"

"Why isn't he/she working for you any longer?"

Then, ask about whatever specifics are important to you, such as honesty, safety, and personal habits.

Most people will answer fairly honestly, but they won't come out directly and say something negative. If your listening skills are carefully tuned, you'll learn a great deal about this candidate by listening between the lines.

Interviewing a Mother-Substitute

These are my personal recommendations:

- Your child should be in the room during the interview (or at least a part of it). You will learn more from the rapport and interaction between the child and the prospective sitter than you will from the interview itself.
- Age of the applicant is important to consider; do you prefer energy or maturity? Is there a language barrier?
- Before you hire anyone to work in your home, you should be sure you are properly insured. You are responsible for any accidents that might occur. Check your homeowner policy to see if it is sufficient. If not, make sure to get adequate coverage because *you are liable!*
- Social Security is another important detail. Frankly, although it is not unheard-of to pay a sitter in cash, it is not only unfair to the person hired, but it is illegal to forego paying Social Security taxes. If you deduct the expense of child care, this could easily be checked, and, again, you are liable.*

QUESTIONS	*REASON*
• Why do you need the job?	Need often determines reliability as well as interest in succeeding.
• What other responsibilities do you have?	Your child must be first.
• What are your attitudes toward raising children?	Discuss interviewee's ideas at length before even mentioning your own. You do not want lip-service agreement. You want to find out how they feel about child raising so that their decisions will be similar to your own.

*"Appendix 2; Legal Responsibilities to Household Employees," page 254.

QUESTIONS	*REASON*
• Are you willing to do any of the following household chores when you are not busy meeting the children's needs? (see Daily Help examples, pp. 108–109)	Nonhousekeepers might be willing to choose certain tasks for which they would be responsible.
• What is your experience?	Check reputation and references for honesty, reliability, and attitudes.
• Can you transport the child as well as yourself?	It may be necessary for the child to go places when you are at work; you might not be able to provide transportation for either your sitter or your children.
• Are you available to sleep over if I am out of town on business or vacation?	Even if it isn't a necessity, it's a great convenience.
• Do you have any health problems? Discuss this in detail, and if the individual is perfectly healthy announce how pleased you are because in no way can you afford to hire anyone who *might* call in sick for anything less than a dire emergency. (Trust me, you can eliminate a nightmare by doing this.)	The job is just too important to give to someone whose health problems might interfere. Also, it is wise not to consider a person who might call you at 7:00 A.M. complaining of a backache or headache.

QUESTIONS	*REASON*
• Are you willing to follow a daily schedule and include my recommended daily activities as part of your work day?	A daily plan helps ensure that you won't end up with a preschool TV addict. It also gives clear-cut guidelines of what activities you want for your child.

If the idea of setting up a required schedule rubs you the wrong way, or if you feel it sounds too rigid to plan a schedule, let me say that twenty years ago, when my friend Maida and I were young mothers discussing child care and she told me she left a lesson plan for the sitter, I thought it was unnecessary. Then, when I discovered that my sitter was plopping my precious, precocious toddler in front of television reruns all day, I realized that Maida had a good idea. Her children always had a morning activity such as taking a walk in nice weather, or making clay with flour and water when it rained, or simply learning to put the blocks neatly into the box. Whatever you feel is appropriate for your child to do should be explained to and expected to be followed by your sitter as part of the job description.

SAMPLE DAILY PLAN FOR MOTHER OR MOTHER-SUBSTITUTE

This plan is very tight, and perhaps you would prefer to plan by the hour instead of by the half-hour time.

Time	Activity
8:30–9:00 A.M.	Breakfast Talking time
9:00–9:30 A.M.	Bathing Dressing
9:30–10:00 A.M.	Make bed Straighten room

Time	Activity
10:00–11:00 A.M.	Morning activity*
11:00–11:30 A.M.	Snack Story time
11:30–12:00 Noon	Fruit time Prepare lunch
12:00–12:45 P.M.	Lunch Children nap
12:45–1:00 P.M.	Straighten kitchen
1:00–2:00 P.M.	Laundry Iron
2:00–2:30 P.M.	Snack Talking time
2:30–3:30 P.M.	Activity*
4:00–4:30 P.M.	Start supper Set table
4:30–5:00 P.M.	Quiet time

In the space that follows try to make your own daily plan. Consider what you need and want your helper to do with your child(ren) or for your household while you are at work.

Time	*Activity*
____________________	____________________
	____________________
____________________	____________________
	____________________
____________________	____________________
	____________________

*Decide on an appropriate activity according to age and interest of the child, for example, gather leaves, watch educational TV programs, water plants, do puzzles, listen to records, bake cookies, or nap.

Time	*Activity*
______________	______________
	______________
______________	______________
	______________
______________	______________
	______________
______________	______________
	______________
______________	______________
	______________
______________	______________
	______________
______________	______________
	______________

Step Seven: Reevaluation

I will reevaluate my child-care decision in ________ weeks/months/semester/duration of job span.

If noticeable changes take place or when something stops working I will:

STOP

ASK WHY

1. Why isn't it working?
2. Why is my child unhappy?
3. Why am I not content?
4. Why isn't the mother-substitute content?

MAKE CHANGES

1. What changes might benefit your child?
2. What changes will make you

more comfortable with your mother-substitute?

3. How can you prepare your children to adapt to these changes?

TRY ANOTHER ALTERNATIVE

1. There are no simple solutions, only intelligent choices.

The relationship between an employer and an employee, particularly when the employer's children are involved, is a very personal one. These relationships, which on the average change about every eighteen months, can last longer and be more rewarding if clear expectations and open communication go hand in hand. So, while evaluating anything that went wrong, consider how communication contributed to making the relationship good or bad.

Here are a few more points to consider as well.

What Child Care Personnel Expect from Parents

No matter what the individual partnership agreement is between you and the people who care for your child(ren), one thing is sure: they have expectations, too!

Fiscal responsibility means pay on time. One woman who has cared for five children at a time in her home for thirteen years expressed this common problem best: "It's still a business, and I count on the money at the end of the week. When children don't come on Thursday or Friday, parents often don't bother to drop off the money, which I depend on for groceries. I don't think it's fair for me to have to wait until Monday to get paid. They expect their salary on time, and so do I."

Phone the sitter if necessary. If a child is *not* coming, or will be out for a few days, call the sitter and inform her of your schedule.

Give yourself leeway, but be prompt. If you have to be late picking up your child, call and explain. If you have a job that doesn't end at a fixed time, it is advisable to have your child expect you later in the day, rather than earlier. It is far healthier for the child—even if most days you use the extra time to exercise, enjoy an after-work cool-down period, do chores, or run errands—than to wait anxiously at the window worried about when (if?) you will arrive.

Consider the other children. If your child comes down with a contagious disease, make sure you have backup emergency care if you can't stay home with him/her. It is best to have a family member or person close to the child be there, but as a last (and expensive) resort, you could call a nursing care agency.

Better to buy a modest gift for each child in the group than to have one child showing off something extravagant that the others could never have.

Keep your expectations reasonable. Not many sitters will do extra tasks like chauffeuring the children. If you need transportation, discuss it, but don't be surprised if you are asked to find other means of transporting your child from the sitter's to ballet class.

Be involved and participate. Make sure you understand exactly what is expected of you and that your obligations are reasonable. It is better to make your objections and inabilities clear at the outset than to fail to meet expectations set for you. Innovative mothers (and most working mothers get "A" for innovation every time), manage to work reasonable activities into their impossible schedules. For example, if you can *never* participate in a daily event at the location where the children are, perhaps you can arrange to invite the group to your workplace for an outing. At the very least, show interest!

WHAT EVERY BABY-SITTER SHOULD KNOW ABOUT YOUR CHILD

Nickname:
Age:
Particular Dislikes:
Allergies:
Parents can be reached at: (h) (o)
Emergency Contacts:
- Family Member:
- Doctor:
- Hospital Emergency Room:
- Fire Department:
- Police (ambulance):

FAVORITE:
- Toys:
- Foods:
- Snacks:
- TV programs:
- Books:

SCHEDULE:
- Naptime:
- Bedtime:
- Bathtime:
- Bathroom habits:
- Rituals:
- Specific instructions:

HOUSEHOLD MANAGEMENT

OF the myriad problems confronting the mother who works both at home and in the marketplace, the day-to-day running of the household looms high as the major difficulty. Management of the household is a two-part problem for the wage-earning mother, composed of child care and housekeeping.

Until you find the right child care, nothing else matters. But once you've found good child care, household management becomes one of the most important points to consider if you are, or are planning to become, a working mother. With child care the number one priority, often costing more than they can afford, most mothers are left with the aggravation of keeping up with the household chores. Recurring complaints are voiced by working mothers who come home from work to go to work. This is just one of the most typical: "He comes home before I do and sits down with his feet up and the newspaper in his hand. I rush home an hour later because I've stopped to do three errands and race into the kitchen to start dinner."

Surveys and reports reinforce what I've learned from working mothers: few have much help with household management. On

January 12, 1982, a *Newsday* article reported on a working mother magazine survey. It said: "Eight of ten husbands were supportive of their wife's return to work after the baby's birth, but only one-third of the women said their spouses helped a lot with housework." The *Ladies Home Journal* conducted a study at about the same time I was interviewing working women for this book. I quote it because it reinforces what I learned from answers to questionnaires as well as personal interviews: "Three-fifths of the women (including part-timers) work outside the home, but, on the average, 86% of these women also carry all, or almost all, of the responsibilities for cleaning, laundry, and cooking. Women also handle more than 70% of the child care and the grocery shopping. Fifty-five percent take care of finances and pay the bills."

One of the realities shared among working mothers is the knowledge that only mothers are usually willing to do both child care and housekeeping chores. Once it becomes necessary to pay someone to do these jobs, one finds that they usually require two entirely different job descriptions. Often, two (or more) people have to be hired to do what is fondly referred to as "mother's work."

Unfortunately, few working families can afford to pay for the services of full-time housekeepers. Those of us who dream about hiring a "Mary Poppins," if we could afford her, forget that Mary did not do housework!

Statistically, few working mothers can pay for housekeeping help, for the following reasons:

- Women earn less than 60 percent of a man's wages.
- The number of females as heads of households is increasing.
- Child care uses the available money.

Throughout this text you will see examples of how *attitude* plays a greater role in determining who does what housework than does financial ability.

I interviewed women with full-time, sleep-in housekeepers. Most of these women did every chore at home that they did before getting a job. Even if they never scrubbed the floors, they still continued to do whatever they were used to doing. This included shopping, cooking, serving the meals, and tidying the kitchen. Their housekeepers scrubbed the bathrooms, vacuumed, and ironed, but they rarely cooked, served meals, or assumed any of the myriad other housewifely chores such as caring for plants or pets.

A more recent study, published in the book *American Couples* by Philip Blumstein, Ph.D., and Pepper Schwartz, Ph.D., reaches the following conclusion: "At the present time, many women are employed, but most of the former wifely roles are still in place. Men are working and living with working women, but they resist changing the rules on which their alliance is based. When we look at housework and find that it is still the woman's job, even if she is working full-time, we know that men have not accepted women as true 'partners.' Housework—who does it and how it is divided—is a good barometer of how much further women have yet to go to achieve equity with men."

I quote their conclusions because of the credibility of their research. It was funded by the National Science Foundation and the Russell Sage Foundation. Their in-depth study, conducted in the mid-1970s, includes data from thousands of questionnaires and three hundred interviews in couples' homes. Two years later several thousand couples were surveyed again. Interestingly, the findings of the second study concur with the research upon which this book is based and which was conducted, on a much smaller scale in 1979. About five hundred working women (many of whom were career-oriented and members of professional organizations) answered questionnaires prepared by psychologist Maida Berenblatt. Then I interviewed at least a hundred more women. The conclusion I reached—working women come home from work to start working—inspired this book: YOU CAN'T DO IT ALL. Blumstein and Schwartz say it this way: "Working wives still bear almost all the responsibility for housework."

A *New York Times* poll about women and work reported that 55 percent of women and 70 percent of men think that husbands should do half of the cleaning. The discrepancy between what husbands should do, however, and what they actually do is vast. Typically, full-time working wives spend thirty hours per week on household chores, more even than unemployed males.

Soon after, on the occasion of the one hundredth anniversary issue of the *Ladies Home Journal,* a special report was published based on the views of eighty-six thousand readers. Entitled "Portrait of the American Woman Today," by Clive Enos, Ph.D., and Sondra Forsyth Enos, it reported:

- 89 percent have no paid help (personal incomes under $30,000)
- 75 percent have no paid help (personal incomes over $30,000)
- 71 percent argue most about house rules and chores

And just so you know other women feel the same way, here are the top answers to two questions.

Question #1: What makes women angry?
Answer: When I have to pick up after everybody else.
Question #2: What is most likely to make women feel depressed?
Answer: When everybody is making too many demands on me.

Among the readers in the *Ladies Home Journal* poll, 71 percent had children and 72 percent worked outside the home. Among the general public, according to the United States Census Bureau (1980), 56 percent of mothers with children under age eighteen and 48 percent of mothers with children under age six are in the labor force. It is easy to conclude that many of these mothers do most of their own housework. A *New York Times* article, which I clipped on November 3, 1976, had this startling headline: "75% of Women Physicians in Detroit Survey Report They Do Housework, Too."

I think you'll agree that neither the wives with housekeepers nor the physicians did their own housework for financial reasons. I'd be surprised to learn that they did it because they enjoyed it. Why, then, do you suppose they did it? I suggest that they did it either because they wanted to be in control or because they felt guilty. Attitude, rather than finances, determined their choices!

Meanwhile, single mothers on limited funds often have no difficulty delegating their housework chores effectively. Why? One reason is that they have so much responsibility that they feel no loss of control. Another is that they have no alternative to working, so they feel no guilt! I don't envy their position, but I admire their achievements. They certainly manage their households skillfully!

People who choose to do everything themselves often suffer from physical stress symptoms, such as headaches, migraines, ulcers, or fatigue. This tells me that it's necessary to reduce stress as much as possible, particularly at home, where it really *can* be managed! We should replan, reorganize, and decide how to manage our households so that they run while we're busy. We should share our household responsibilities with everyone who lives there. We should try to stop doing everything ourselves!

You can learn how to manage your household better by applying the many techniques and alternatives used by the women in this book. If you learn this skill *before* beginning your career, you will be years ahead of other working mothers who fumbled and juggled and nagged (and cried) until they got cooperation.

You can try to combine a career with motherhood, love, relationships, and a workable household. Lots of people do it successfully. *But you can't do it all just because it all has to get done!*

Most of all, if *your* attitude changes, and *you* understand how important it is for *your* mental and physical health *not* to come home from work to do everything, *your* future life will be more satisfying.

Each anecdote that follows illustrates one personal style in a wage-earning mother's approach to household management. They are divided into four categories:

- The Supermom
- The Typical Salaried Mother
- The Administrator
- The Family Team

ROLE MODELS

Supermom

The woman who is off and running in the Supermom marathon is omnipresent, and she has lots of competition. Everyone, it seems, is racing to pass her. If only they could hear me yelling from afar, "Slow down! You're going to hurt yourself! Stop doing everything!"

Supermom does everything. But it isn't what she does that distinguishes her; it is her attitude. Does having a cleaning person exempt the Supermom? Never. Supermom does it all because she basically believes the jobs belong to her. You don't hear her muttering, "It's easier for me to do it than fight about it," while loading the laundry. She doesn't even detest the advertising agency that invented "ring around the collar." If you give her a Seal-A-Meal, she keeps it in a closet because it would never occur to her to avoid washing pots.

My children used to remind me that what was wrong with me was that I didn't understand that "real mothers" are supposed to be Supermoms, because. . . .

Supermom's Children Come First

- Supermoms spend their salaries on their children.
- Supermoms are always available to drive.
- Supermoms prepare the meal, set the table, and serve their children *before* going out to dinner.
- Supermoms never feel guilty about dumping their children's drawers in the middle of the floor because Supermom matches the socks and keeps the child's drawers tidy herself! (I've been told that some Supermoms actually enter the bedrooms of their teenaged offspring, clean up, open and straighten inside bureau drawers, pick up laundry, vacuum, dust, straighten, and leave. Naturally, Supermom's children never ever complain about "personal privacy" or "infringement of basic human rights." After all, these kids know when they have it made!)
- Supermoms do their daily chores early, before work and while the rest of the family sleeps. They pick up, clean up, scrub, launder, wash, cook, and then leave for "work."

Supermom Doesn't Expect Help

- Supermom doesn't expect her husband to participate fully because his work is more
  a. important
  b. financially rewarding
  c. exhausting
  d. all of the above
- Supermom doesn't expect her children to share the chores because
  a. her mother did it for her
  b. schoolwork is enough to handle
  c. they'd never do it "right" anyway
  d. all of the above

- Supermom doesn't hire out any household chores, even when there is enought money, because
  a. a woman's job is to care for the family
  b. her husband doesn't want a *stranger* in the house
  c. it's easier to do it herself
  d. all of the above

Supermom: Sally

So many women are Supermoms that choosing just one life to illustrate is difficult. I could mention three Supermoms who don't ever have to do housework, but they do it anyway. (They have full-time help!)

But the person most worthy of the title "Supermom" is the eldest daughter of a large family who learned early the rewards of pleasing others. Her name is Sally, and today she combines her professional and personal lives in a style that makes her a Supermom.

Sally does everything for her family. Rarely is she free for an afternoon or evening; she never makes plans without first checking with everybody. And at her job at the local beauty parlor, she does more than her share. Once I heard that when she left a job, her boss had to hire three people to replace her.

Sally and I went to high school together. After high school, she became a manicurist and continued working at home during the evenings while her babies were young. (Today, working mothers come to your home and do your nails and hair, bringing their babies with them.) Later, during their early school years, she worked weekends and evenings.

Through the years, she accumulated licenses as a skin care person, as a cosmetologist, and finally as a beautician. Her ultimate goal is to own a shop.

Sally did my hair on New Year's Eve. At the shop on New Year's Eve there's a hum in the air, a bottle of wine, and a partylike atmosphere. The place bustles with people preparing for the night's festivities. When Sally started telling me about her annual New Year's Eve sit-down dinner for thirty, I knew I was listening to Supermom. It never occurred to her that she had chosen the busiest day of her professional career to present her fantastic dinner party. So Sally Supermom strives.

She listed all the shopping errands she did after work. She told me how she spent all day Sunday cleaning the house and how she prepared ahead so there would be less for her to do when she got home.

Her menu, which included paella and required many fresh ingredients, was impressive. Each detail was discussed: "First, I cut up the lobster, precook it, flash freeze it, and then it is ready for tonight when I put it all together."

If one can be exhausted while relaxing at the hairdresser's, one can be exhausted listening to Sally. Need I elaborate on the recipe? Or the rest of the menu? Suffice it to say, Supermom chooses the most difficult way rather than the easiest. Her shopping and cleaning done, her table set, her sauces simmering and hors d'oeuvres chilling, Sally Supermom is on her feet, working a ten-hour day.

She did mention that it would have been wonderful if her husband or teenaged children had helped, but their appreciation seems to be enough. Does an accountant change offices on April 14? Do letter carriers volunteer to transport trees at Christmastime? Do retailers go on family vacations during Christmas and Easter? No, but Sally Supermom prepares a dinner party on the busiest work day of the year!

Why do some people put down the Supermom in our society? Not because she doesn't deserve praise for her achievements. Not because she doesn't do everything better than most. Mostly, it is because

- *Supermom* is the woman in the articles about harmful stress.
- *Supermom* is Type A, the one who gets heart attacks.
- *Supermom* runs to the doctor with stress-related symptoms.
- *Supermom* might change the longevity statistics.

And, if truth be known, Supermom is the mother of all those sons in the world who believe it is their birthright to come home from work, put their feet up, and have their socks picked up, dinner ready promptly at six, and the children driven to the movies. And you know who is supposed to do it!

Moreover, magazines keep telling us how to be Supermom, and I don't believe that is the answer. Books on the market try to convince us that if we get up earlier, run to fill our children's needs during lunchtime, and stay up later, we, too, can do it all.

If you tell a Supermom that she does it all because she needs to be needed, she frequently responds, "Oh! no, I love taking care of them."

If Supermom reads that she creates dependency on herself by totally filling her family's needs, she'll deny it.

Supermom doesn't know she's compulsive. But when Supermom feels physical discomforts and loses that all-over feeling of well-being, she begins to question the logic of her meticulous devotion.

Unfortunately, for some Supermoms it is too late to change the family's expectations. Readjustment to shared family responsibilities often takes more effort than it is worth. It may even destroy the family unit. Some Supermoms are stuck!

So, if being a Supermom is still your chosen style, give up smoking and prepare for endurance. Eat right, get your exercise, and take vitamin pills. Supermoms need all the strength they can muster.

Typical Salaried Mother (TSM): A Day in the Life

TSM gets up very early. She showers, letting the water flow on her wash-and-wear hair. (She has no time for weekly wash and sets; one cut every six weeks is typical.) She chooses one of her workday uniforms, skirt, blouse, and tailored jacket. She tries to look feminine, of course, but sexy—never! She starts the coffee, throws in a load of laundry, and takes something out of the freezer to defrost for dinner. She tries to wake the children to spend some precious minutes with them, but they'd rather sleep. Often, she bundles a little one to take to the sitter. In the car she applies lipstick and, wearing sunglasses, saves putting on makeup for her morning coffee break.

Work? Every TSM's day is unique but shares one certainty: the nothing-to-do-with-the-job phone calls. During the day, every TSM will place a call that sounds something like this:

- Orthodontist: "Tommy's brace broke—*again*."
- Garage: "The starter sounds funny. . . ."
- Service people: "The dishwasher flooded, the dryer is cold. . . ."
- Husband: "I have a late meeting—can you get the dry-cleaning?"
- Sitter: "I forgot to tell you that Sarah has a doctor's appointment."

And then, at about three, there's *the call*. Mothers around the world call home after school. This call ties up switchboards in corporations. It's the call that assures each Typical Salaried Mother that her darling children survived getting off to school and that they arrived home safely. Latent fears of emergency dissipate with this assurance, and sighs of relief abound when mothers at the office learn that Tommy is yelling and Nancy is crying because Judy changed the channel.

After work, on her way home, TSM's mind is busy, not with new ideas to present at tomorrow's sales meeting, but checking off the list of errands: the bank? (too late), the cleaners? (tomorrow), milk? (forgot to ask), car pool? (Oh! damn, it's Tuesday).

Home! Time for the children! Dinner time! Have you noticed that TSM's children are the only deprived children in America? Sustained on McDonald's, Pizza Hut, and Kentucky Fried Chicken, they are deprived of homemade—unless, of course, TSM loves to cook and believes in wok-prepared veggies and homemade soups; then her children are the only ones deprived of junk food as a standard diet.

The men in our lives come home, dreaming about sheer nighties and chilled martinis, and find themselves helping with dinner and doing the dishes. They have become confused about the vast difference between their early expectations and their daily reality.

The evening hours, once reserved for grown-ups and romance, are shared by a cast of loved ones:

- TSM wants to make love.
- TSM wants to help the children.
- TSM wants to see her friends.
- TSM wants to support community activities.
- TSM wants to do it all.

Instead, she puts away the laundry or reacts to whoever needs her most. Then she prepares for the morrow and collapses.

One more important thing about TSM: *she wouldn't have it any other way.*

Typical Salaried Mother may sound like a Supermom to you readers. But she is not. She expects help around the house. In fact, she asks for it. But when cooperation is not forthcoming, she often does it herself, muttering all the while, "It's easier to do it than fight about it. . . ."

TSM often asks her children to do their chores, but if Jane leaves the clothes in the washer, she kindly throws them into the dryer, thinking (naively perhaps) that Jane will notice, throw her arms around her in appreciation, and offer to do something special! But such scenes, fantasies from commercial land, rarely occur at home. Instead, Jane keeps forgetting, TSM keeps doing, and, very unlike Supermom, recognizes and resents it.

We TSMs will be asking, begging, pleading, and yelling forever if we keep expecting *them* to help *us*. As long as we are asking them to help us they, correctly, see the jobs as belonging to us. So, unless we really want to do everything forevermore, we must teach our families that the jobs are everyone's to share.

INTERACTION

Do you identify with the Typical Salaried Mother?

"Would you bring in the garbage pails?"
"Sally, please fold the laundry."
"Will you please help me set the table?"
"Honey, could you please pick up Steven on your way home?"
"Mary, when will you finish these dishes. . . "
"Would you???"
"Could you???"
"Please help me!"

If these comments sound familiar, then you can identify with the role of the Typical Salaried Mother. The next question to ask yourself is: How do you feel when you say these things?

WHO ARE YOU?

Do you feel good about yourself and the other members of your family when you ask them for help? If yes, then it is working for you. You have your act together. If not, let's explore further to determine how you feel when you ask for help from your family.

Do you feel

- *sorry for yourself*
  when/if ______________________________
- *hostile* at other's lack of consideration
  when/if ______________________________
- *discouraged*
  when/if ______________________________
- *angry*
  when/if ______________________________
- *alone* in your concern for your home
  when/if ______________________________
- *helpless*
  when/if ______________________________

INTERACTION

After you have determined which of the previous feelings best describes you, fill in the typical dialogues between yourself and other family members.

Situation #1 Dirty dishes in sink

What *you* say: ____________________

____

What *they* say: ____________________

____

Situation #2 No socks match

What *you* say: ____________________

____

What *they* say: ____________________

____

Situation #3 The bathroom is a wreck

What *you* say: ____________________

____

What *they* say: ____________________

____

For further exploration, determine the following:

1. Is there a pattern in your answers? ______
2. Is there a pattern in their responses? ______
3. Is there a relationship between your feelings (as determined on p. 65) and the pattern in your answers? ______
4. Is it possible that the approach you have chosen for household management is not working? ______
5. Is there friction? ______
6. Is there frustration? ______
7. Is there anger? ______
8. Is there stress? ______
9. Are you willing to experiment with the role of administrator? ______

10. Are you willing to experiment with other alternatives? ______
11. Would your family be interested in the family team approach? ______

Believe me, I *know* how very difficult it is to make changes. It is especially difficult when the changes require the cooperation of other people. But is it really easier to stay with a situation that is not working? Other members of your family may even welcome an opportunity to try another way. In any case, you have little to lose, considering the ineffectiveness of the present method.

A helpful approach to a cooperative change is to stop using an ineffective method. Perhaps nothing will change but your attitude. But if your attitude changes, if you learn to think of family matters as *everyone's* responsibility, not just yours, you may feel better about yourself and, consequently, you may be able to reduce your anxiety, anger, frustration, and stress.

The Administrator

Administrators are people most of us recognize. They organize and manage their households by using techniques similar to those used in business.

Unlike the Supermom, the Administrator makes no attempt to do all the chores herself; rather, she assumes the ultimate responsibility for seeing to it that tasks are assigned and completed.

Her job includes

- Delegation of tasks
- Hiring or asking for help
- Ultimate responsibility

The Administrator: Pam

Double the trouble, double the fun!

Last year was the time for twins: two friends of mine, both in their thirties, gave birth to twins. Being a working mother of twin infants is not easy.

Pam is a very together woman. She is professional, efficient, intelligent, and charming. While busily climbing her career ladder, she keeps her cool, recognizes the obstacles, and copes with the problems. Blond and feminine, she combines the strength of Goliath with the cleverness of David.

Her first marriage was a disaster. She left, with her daughter and a teaching degree, to make a better life for herself. She never received a dime in alimony or child support, and the father never attempted to see his child.

Pam returned home, and, for the next seven years, she worked and concentrated on accumulating the credentials necessary to create her future career. She became certified as a guidance counselor, then as a principal. Now, she is an assistant superintendent of schools.

She sacrificed personal privacy for the emotional security living with her family would give her child. By keeping her living expenses low, she was able to afford music and gymnastic lessons and other luxuries. The child accompanied Pam as much as possible, and Pam dated a man who happily included her child when they went to the beach, the movies, and other activities.

Today her life includes many other roles; she is the mother of twins and an adolescent, the wife of a banker, and the manager of a substantial home as well as a career woman who spends long hours committed to her work.

Her husband, who went from bachelorhood to fatherhood, from few responsibilities to many, has few hours to help at home. He commutes a long distance, travels regularly, and spends a great amount of time and energy on his career. He is enormously supportive of his wife's ambition and her career problems and has taken days off from work to take his sick children to the doctor. He enjoys spending time with the children and finds time for certain specific responsibilities at home, but he prefers that his wife be the business manager of the home front. As a professional administrator, Pam uses many of her career skills to organize the management of her home.

Rule #1: You Can't Do It All

The Administrator understands that it is not her job to do everything, and she does not expect to do it all. Nor is it her job to do work that belongs to other people. Since she is ultimately responsible for seeing that everything gets done, she is often willing to eliminate low-priority items. These vary from family to family. For some, it might mean boxing the silver or the sets of tea cups that collect dust. For others, it means living with a dirty oven or eating prepared foods. For still others, it means eliminating the flower garden or the weekend guests that used to provide pleasure but have become a chore. For some of us, it means closing our eyes from Monday to Friday and buying new stockings when none are clean!

Rule #2: If It Can Be Delegated, Delegate It

Delegating is as simple as keeping a list for the teenaged baby-sitter, who, instead of watching TV when children are sleeping, might be willing to earn a few extra dollars by doing the following chores:

- Wrap a present
- Peel the potatoes
- Trim a tree
- Empty ashtrays
- Fold laundry
- Prepare a salad
- Take out trash
- Sew on buttons

Although most sitters or mother-substitutes automatically refuse to do housework, there are many chores that some people will do happily. Find out what your helper or sitter likes to do and assess his or her willingness to do those things for you. Remember, your admiration and appreciation are worth as much as or more than the extra pay.

Believe it or not, I once had a neighbor who *loved* to iron baby clothes but hated to cook. At the age of twenty, I made one of my best barters: I cooked double and she ironed!

A former favorite mother's helper (who drove) loved to shop and to clip coupons. The pennies she saved paid for the hour it took her to shop. She collected the stamps (or cash register receipt for gifts) and I didn't have to run for tuna, toilet paper, or toothpaste after work.

My friend Amy has a grandmotherly sitter who gladly sews on buttons, hems, and does the mending, but who wouldn't dream of cleaning. I have had mother's helpers who loved to shop, others who brought clothes to the cleaners, another who liked to tend plants. One cleaning woman was so proud of her sauces and stews that on the one day a week she cleaned our home I came home to a crockpot simmering with our dinner.

It is important to determine what jobs a sitter will or will not do when you interview. Although your major concern is always child care, you can hire someone lovable and caring who will also help *you* while your children sleep, do homework, watch TV, or play.

I am consistently amazed at the working mothers who tell me about the salaries they pay to mother-substitutes who do not do any chores. Again and again, acquaintances lament, "I was so worried I just wanted to be sure someone was there for them." Of course, but while an afternoon sitter tends to school-age children doing their homework, can't she start the dinner, fold the laundry or do something else to lighten your burden?

Rule #3: The Cost of Good Help Is Part of the Overhead

Administrators are aware that competent help costs money. They also know how difficult it is to locate and keep good workers. Therefore, when they find someone who does the job well, they are willing to pay more. Housework is no exception. As with most services, you get what you pay for. So, if you pay the minimum salary you might not get the maximum results.

There are certain standard costs that vary according to location and date. For that reason, I'll give you my basic formula for payment, but you can find the current pay scale by looking in the classified section of your local newspaper under "Household Help Wanted" or "Situations Wanted."

My formula includes my own abbreviations: GR = going rate (this might be more than—even double or triple—minimum wage), H = hours, X = extras (this includes food, transportation, Social Security, benefits), $ = dollars spent, x = times. Therefore, my formula looks like this: $GR \times H + X = \$$. Translated into English it means: The going rate times the number of hours plus the extra costs equals the dollars spent.

Remember, this cost is part of your overhead! Like taxes, it must be paid, and it usually hurts.

Rule #4: On-the-Job Training Must Be Completed before You Judge Competency

How many times have you heard people put down their mates or their children, or even the hired help, for not doing things the way they want them done? Do you recognize these quotes:

"If George did the shopping all we'd eat is junk!"
"When Don did the wash once, he threw in my silk blouse with the white wash."
"My sitter cooked dinner last Friday and nobody would eat it."
"I wouldn't mind it if they didn't leave such a mess."

The Administrator knows how to give productive criticism without destroying ambition, without "putting down," and by always starting with an approving thought. If working mothers used that technique and trained their families, then added corrections when necessary, more families would participate in doing the chores.

START ON-THE-JOB TRAINING YOUNG—THE EARLIER THE BETTER*

Training starts at home by doing things together. It is as important a lesson in a home with a housekeeper (will someone always be there to pick up after your child?) as in a home with no helpers. Like the Administrator, your attitude will determine your child's willingness to participate. So, smile and try these "on-the-job" ideas:

- Play "Ring Around the Tub." Teach tots to spray or scrub and bathtime will end with a clean tub.
- Play "fetch" with children. If you can teach dogs to find things, why wait while children hunt for lost shoes? Encourage your children to know where things are and to find them. Perhaps this counting game will help: How many seconds will it take you to find (a) your library book? (b) your raincoat? (c) your puzzles?
- Train youngsters to separate white from colored wash, to match socks, to fold laundry, and to put things away.
- Encourage them to be junior "buspersons" at mealtime.
- Teach them how to use machines and supervise them when they do it. Eight-year-olds can play "laundromat."
- Buy a Dustbuster and let them play with it as if it were a toy. It's small enough for little hands, safe to use, and a perfect household tool. They might even fight for a turn to pick up the crumbs!

*See pages 198–99 for other chores even a toddler can handle.

Rule #5: Reasonable Expectations Help Determine Who Does What!

It is important when you delegate tasks to have expectations geared to the person's

- Age
- Time availability
- Talent
- Degree of distaste

Sex, by the way, usually should *not* be a determining factor. You would not believe how many of my fourteen-year-old students still do chores according to strict stereotypical sexist assignments.

Contrary to common custom, boys can make beds, spread butter, and start washing machines. Boys who operate ten-speed bikes, drive sports cars, and use computers like pros seem to many mothers incapable of pushing buttons on the dishwasher or turning a knob on the washing machine!

Likewise, young women (who still make their brothers' beds) rarely carry out the garbage or mow lawns. Our children will be buying and reading books like this one to help teach them how to share household management unless we teach them to participate equally while they are young.

Rule #6: Your Attitude Determines Their Cooperation

Administrators with helpful, cooperative, and hardworking staffs have an attitude that brings out the best in people. They also use similar techniques at home and at work.

On the job the Administrator:

- Motivates
- Trains and teaches

- Hires and fires
- Organizes and keeps files
- Maintains a pleasant environment
- Identifies strengths and weaknesses
- Delegates
- Keeps supplies available
- Anticipates needs
- Rewards with or denies privileges

At home the Administrator:

- Motivates
- Trains and teaches
- Hires and fires
- Organizes and keeps files
- Maintains a pleasant environment
- Identifies strengths and weaknesses
- Delegates
- Keeps supplies available
- Anticipates needs
- Rewards with or denies privileges

Rule #7: Purchase Time- and Labor-Saving Devices

The Administrator is also aware of the importance of time- and energy-saving devices. She budgets for them, knowing that the investment will pay off in energy saved. This brings me to my microwave tale. While I was interviewing a highly successful woman, whose powerful and prestigious job has been noted in news articles about women who have made it in the male world, our conversation turned to household management. From her, I learned that career women who earn lots of money and who don't have children don't share our problems. But because she and her husband work in different cities and she commutes from Manhattan to their home on weekends, she had a different set of problems. She spoke about the value of a microwave oven for her particular lifestyle. Neither partner wanted to eat in a restaurant when they had so few meals together. Neither felt much like cooking either. Broiled steaks and chops are their answer. A freezer full of food, a microwave oven used only to defrost, and *voila!* They have created an easy private dinner for two.

Since my oven had recently died and I had about half the money I needed for a microwave, I was determined to save up and wait. One full season later, I accumulated the money for my microwave top oven and self-cleaner below. I rarely budget and save for such items. But my microwave was worth it!

I rarely cook a full meal in it, but since I always cook double or triple recipes, portions can be reheated whenever anyone cares to eat. With a Seal-A-Meal to freeze in and a microwave to defrost, even my husband can (after twenty years) find something other than peanuts for dinner!

Here are some time- and labor-saving devices to ease the working mother's life:

- Washing machine and dryer
- Dishwasher
- Microwave oven
- Self-cleaning oven
- Seal-A-Meal
- Dustbuster
- Food processor
- Trash compactor
- Garbage disposal
- Commercial bucket with attached wringer
- Step stool
- Crockpot
- Built-in vacuum cleaner
- Under cabinet appliances

WHO DOES THE CHORES?

Daily Tasks	*Who Does It in Your House?*	*Who Does It in Pam the Administrator's House*
1. Bedrooms		
a. Your own	________	Pam
b. Child's	________	Does own
c. Baby's	________	Baby-sitter
2. Meal preparation		
a. Breakfast	________	Pam does own
1. Prepare		Baby-sitter does the
2. Serve		children's
3. Clean up		
b. Lunch	________	Pam does own
1. Prepare		Baby-sitter does the
2. Serve		children's
3. Clean up		
c. Snack	________	Individual responsibility
d. Dinner		
1. Prepare	________	Rotate among family
2. Serve	________	Pam
3. Clean up	________	Rotate
3. Laundry	________	Each person does own Sitter for young ones
4. Straighten house	________	Everyone
5. Bathrooms	________	Assigned
6. Errands	________	Shared

Weekly Chores	*Who Does It in Your House?*	*Who Does It in Pam the Administrator's House*
1. Change linens	________	Hired help
2. Vacuum and dust	________	Hired help
3. Scrub bath(s)	________	Hired help
4. Plan meals and shop	________	Pam
5. Wash and wax floors	________	Hired help

Weekly Chores	*Who Does It in Your House?*	*Who Does It in Pam the Administrator's House*
6. Polish	__________	Hired help
7. Cook in quantity	__________	The best cook in family
8. Lawn and plant care	__________	Mate/child/Pam

Monthly Chores	*Who Does It in Your House?*	*Who Does It in Pam the Administrator's House*
1. Bulk-food shopping	__________	Family
2. Family-needs shopping	__________	One-on-one outing (One parent and one child)
3. Silver polishing	__________	Child(ren)
4. Furniture polishing	__________	Child(ren)
5. Heavy-duty cleaning	__________	Family/housekeeper

REMEMBER:

- The Administrator does not do everything; she sees to it that jobs get done.
- When the Administrator has announced that grocery needs must be listed or they won't be bought, she does not then run out and buy the much-needed (though unlisted) cream rinse, shaving lotion, or peanut butter.
- When the Administrator has to pick up things that someone left lying around, she boxes whatever is found and stores it for a month.

The Administrator, soft-spoken or not, is often a toughie when she does not get cooperation. In effect, at home, the Administrator denies the equivalent of raises at the office when cooperation is not forthcoming. Otherwise, the Administrator, like most of us, would end up doing it all.

The Family Team Approach: Old Idea, New Adaptation

The Family Team Approach to household management has a long, established history in our country. Readers who are familiar with the large, old-fashioned family or the extended family remember that mother was never expected to do everything. Family members all had their own chores. Little ones cleared the table, older siblings bathed babies and did dishes, grandparents tended to cooking and children's needs, and often both parents had to struggle to survive.

In the recent past, smaller families became more prevalent and technological advances made time-saving devices more affordable. Fewer children were expected to work in their early years. Mom, in her efforts to become the ideal homemaker, often added more and more responsibilities to her job.

Now, Mom is a full- or part-time wage-earning parent with fewer hours available for homemaking. With 86 percent of wage-earning mothers still doing everything at home, Mom is under pressure to find a better way. She owes it to herself to appraise and perhaps adopt the Family Team Approach.

We can identify with the Typical Salaried Mother (frequently by looking in the mirror), and we can recognize the Supermom (look around you), and we can admire the efficiency of the Administrator (even if she's less of a softie than we are), but most of us realize that we don't know many families that operate as a team.

Actually, we may know many families that cooperate, chip in, or help out in many marvelous ways, but there is a distinction. In the Family Team Approach the family member preparing dinner is not helping Mommy. The family member doing the laundry is not doing his sister a favor. The family member weeding the garden is not doing Dad's work. Each is contributing to the well-being of the group.

Although this approach is communal in nature, it is *attitudinal* as well. In fact, in households where the Family Team Approach works successfully, it is the attitude of the family members that is most significant in causing success.

Whatever else the attitude includes, it must include this feeling on the part of the mother: *"Housework does not belong only to me just because I am the mother!"*

Family members share the following feelings:

- They feel that mother's work outside the home is of value. Whether the value is economic or not is irrelevant. All members of the family must approve or they won't cooperate.
- They feel that each family member is responsible for fulfilling his or her personal needs as much as possible.
- They all share belief in the following:
  People who eat should clean up afterward.
  People who make messes should straighten them.
  People who dirty clothes should wash them.

Ad infinitum. . . . If they agree on basic precepts, the Family Team Approach can work.

DIFFERENCES BETWEEN THE FAMILY TEAM APPROACH AND OTHER STYLES OF HOUSEHOLD MANAGEMENT:

Let's first recognize the differences between the person who chooses to participate in a Family Team and those who use other, more commonplace, styles of household management.

Supermom	*vs.* Family Team
1. Supermom believes she must do it alone in order to have household chores done properly.	1. The Family Team believes that each member of the group is competent to contribute a fair share.
2. Supermom's high standards reinforce her feelings of self and her importance in the household.	2. The Family Team feels satisfaction from working together to handle chores. Their standards reflect each person's participation.

3. Supermom doesn't ask for help because the jobs belong to her.	3. The Family Team doesn't "help"—they participate in a joint effort for joint benefit.

Typical Salaried Mother	*vs.* Family Team
1. TSM wants her family to help but often finds it easier to do the chores herself than to train, ask, plead, and argue about getting them done.	1. The Family Team lives with undone chores or applies peer pressure until the person responsible does them.
2. TSM perceives that the chores belong to her.	2. The mother in the Family Team does not believe the chores belong to her. She waits and even ignores (it's tough) undone chores.
3. TSM expects her family to help her meet her style of household management.	3. The mother in the Family Team doesn't get involved with style and is satisfied if the style is different than her own.

Administrator	*vs.* Family Team
1. The ultimate responsibility to see that the job gets done belongs to the Administrator.	1. The person in charge of a specific chore is responsible to see to it that it is done.
2. The Administrator has all of the responsibility.	2. The family members share the responsibility.
3. When it isn't working, the Administrator feels all of the pressure.	3. When it isn't working, every member of the family team feels pressure.

The Family Team: Dorothy (We All Come First)

Let me remind you about Dorothy (We All Come First). Her family uses a simplified form of the Family Team Approach. Dorothy contributes her fair share of household chores, but she enjoys the freedom and elimination of work that the Family Team affords. Dorothy, by the way, has no money available for cleaning services after she pays her mother-substitute to take care of the baby. Time for child care is allocated at a weekly family meeting. Whoever is home tends to the baby and takes care of dinner. Consideration is given so the teenager has time to socialize with friends on weekend evenings and to be involved with sports activities.

Because child care and play time are unquestionably the top priority, dinner is simplified as much as possible. Dorothy shops and keeps a supply of easy-to-prepare foods in the house. Dinner chores, from deciding what to eat, to preparation, serving, and cleaning up, are entirely left to the person in charge.

This freedom for Dorothy may not sound like much. But the majority of mothers I know feel they are responsible for making, preparing, and having a meal in the oven before they go anywhere. Frequently, they come home to finish cleaning up the kitchen, too! If the Family Team Approach does nothing more than offer mothers freedom from worrying about a few meals a week, this book is worthwhile.

In Dorothy's home, chores are equitably divided. This does not mean that Dorothy is free of housekeeping responsibilities. On the contrary, she dusts, vacuums, and keeps the kitchen clean. She also does the major food shopping and is responsibile for a few meals a week. Her husband makes his contribution by preparing dinner and caring for their child the two evenings each week that Dorothy attends classes. He does all the family laundry and fetches their "take-out" meals. He also has the unenviable task of finding an appropriate parking space each day. City residents understand how aggravating that chore can be.

The teenager shares in maintaining the household. He baby-sits on nights when both parents are out and helps care for the baby when everyone is at home. He prepares a couple of simple dinners each week and is in charge of cleaning his own bedroom and the family bathroom.

This family team works because

- They all take care of their personal items.
- No one leaves a mess for the next person to clean.
- They share a sense of mutual responsibility.

How The Family Team Approach Works

Concept #1: The Family Group Decides

Before you can even begin to adopt the Family Team Approach, your *family* must agree to these basic concepts. There may be a lot of venting of emotion, but if they agree, you've got it made!

Will your family agree

	YES	*NO*
To cooperate as a team with mutual goals?	_____	_____
To participate equitably?	_____	_____
To assume individual responsibility?	_____	_____
To distribute chores fairly?	_____	_____
To recognize individual differences in style?	_____	_____
To let go of a chore that belongs to someone else?	_____	_____
To participate with equal votes?	_____	_____

Concept #2: Each Individual Owns Certain Responsibilities According to Logical Criteria

Ability. Age (for example, youngsters cannot chauffeur) and natural and acquired talents will help determine who does what jobs.

Time availability. The first person home starts dinner preparation.

Degree of distaste for chore. Who wants to eat a meal prepared by someone who *hates* to cook?

Mutual agreement vs. *individual importance.* If one person in the family wants linen changed twice a week, that person ends up with the job because of its importance to that individual.

Equitable Distribution. Try to even out the chores in an equitable fashion. If parents want children to do most of the chores, either allowance or payment might be increased to make a more equitable distribution or reasonable privileges might be granted.

Concept #3: The Family Group Meets

1. *Discuss what chores need be done.*
2. *Determine who will be responsible for what chores.*
3. *Create a rotating schedule.* Daily, weekly, or monthly plans work. Weekday and weekend plans can work.
4. *Hire out what you can afford to pay for and hate to do.* Neighborhood kids weed, scrub, and clean for money even if your own don't.
5. *Let it go!* See Concept #4.

Concept #4: Let It Go

Believe it or not, many women find it very difficult to give up housewifely chores because it means giving up control and power. This is what I referred to when I mentioned the study of female physicians who do their own housework. Traditionally, women have been excluded from male power bastions. Women have had to use their homes as their primary power base. Now, even though women are achieving success, prestige, and power outside their homes, many continue to remain in control at home.

Unfortunately, until overworked working mothers consider relinquishing some control, they remain responsible for countless chores. For some women, the energy they exert to have everything done their own way is worth doing everything themselves. If, however, you are anxious to relieve yourself of some of the work, you have to be willing to let go of some of the control. Naturally, if the system you are using is working for you, you will not want to change it. But if you are looking for a change and find little cooperation from your family members, the reason probably is that they resent doing everything *your* way. Mothers who are willing to let go of *their* way find themselves free with energy left over to do other things.

The first thing to let go is the expression "my way." One must consider different standards and different styles when one adopts the Family Team Approach. Consider the following examples:

- Your child cooks a vegetarian meal and you prefer meat and potatoes. Your choice is simple. Go back to cooking your way or appreciate your child's creativity and effort.
- Someone ruined a good sweater in the wash. Your way is to use Woolite and cold water. You can yell, scold, or scream *and* do the year's laundry yourself *or* you can chalk up the loss to experience and appreciate that it was only

one item in eight months of not doing the laundry. The choice is yours.

- Your husband tends to the children on his day off. You work that day, and though you prefer home-cooked, healthy foods, your husband's idea of good meals includes Egg McMuffin for breakfast and Kentucky Fried Chicken for lunch. Perhaps when it occurs to him that dressing toddlers in snowsuits is a greater effort than pouring cereal into a dish, your husband will change his style. But so far, neither children nor husband appear to suffer. He enjoys his private day with the youngsters. They love being with him. Wisely, you choose to be quiet rather than interfere, prepare the meals yourself, or talk about "your way." You know when you're well off!
- Your way might include opening the door to your children's room and seeing a room as neat and tidy as one in a magazine picture. But if you can let go of your way and let the children live with anything this side of the health inspector's standards, you will eliminate your anxiety and stress—and you will also save your vocal chords. If your way is very important, you might have to clean the children's room yourself. Supermom doesn't mind doing it. If you do, then try to compromise. In our family the children try to
  a. Keep the door shut so that we won't be offended.
  b. Clean up before important guests visit.
  c. Clean up when they can't stand it anymore!

The second thing to let go is *dinner*. In many personal interviews, women talked about the changes in their daily dinnertime meals. Gourmet delights, seven nights a week, are out. Perhaps the cost of food or the awareness of diet and nutrition plays a role. But the reality is that *nobody* feels like coming home from work to cook a big meal every single night. Delis, fast-food, take-out, frozen, and simplified meals have become a new way of life.

Concept #5: Shared Power among Members of the Family Team
To Relinquish Control = To Lose Power

In traditional styles of household management, power and control were often in the hands of the mother. The Administrator has the power to delegate or to withdraw favors. The Typical Salaried Mother has the power to complain and nag and give guilt. The Supermom has total control because she is willing to do everything to keep the power of having it done her way. But in the Family Team Approach, the power base is shared. Who really has the power in the family? Is anything more powerful than a baby's cry? In a real sense, no one is weaker or stronger than another in the family.

It is this concept of shared power and shared responsibility that makes the family team a satisfying lifestyle. There are no rewards, no punishments, just good feelings of contributing to the family goals.

Concept #6: What to Do When the Family Team Doesn't Function

You can:

- Express anger or disappointment
- Call a family meeting to discuss the problem openly
- Redefine commitments when necessary
- Let it go for a while
- Reschedule job roles

You cannot:

- Do it for them
- Punish
- Bribe
- Reward

The Family Team Approach: Midge

Midge's family has polished and perfected the Family Team Approach. Midge never, ever did housework. Midge was never rich. She worked her way through college and her early married years. When her babies were young, the mother-substitute, one mature woman, did all the laundry and cared for the children. She even followed a lesson plan for daily activities like the one in this book. When she divorced, Midge worked at two or three jobs to support her children and the mother-substitute who cared for them. She continued earning higher degrees.

Her children soon knew what they realistically could expect from their mother. They expected her to have time available to meet their needs. Since her children have recurring health problems, her time and emotional support have always been of paramount importance to them. She is, of course, expected to have food in the house and transportation arranged on days when she works late. Yet the children would never dream, knowing their mother's tight work schedule, of demanding rides at the last minute.

Naturally, the children expect their fair share of comfort and pleasure, and their mother tries very hard to provide them with both. They have grown to be happy, loving, sensible, and successful young people. The children look forward to shared family vacations but accept doing household chores as part of their daily life. They neither resent their responsibilities nor feel anger at having to meet them. They feel this way, I am convinced, because they share equal values and have similar attitudes. They all believe in the concept of shared family responsibilities. Attitude is what makes their family function as a team.

Letting go is not a problem for Midge. For example, it helps that Midge doesn't really care about food. Cooking is neither an art form nor therapy for her; rather, it is the means to prepare a nutritious meal. Thus when one of the children prepares an exotic original dish, Midge is grateful and appreciative of the child's creativity, success, and so on. She does not notice too much garlic or not enough oregano. She doesn't relate to the mess in the kitchen because, obviously, it belongs to the cook. Her attitude protects her from a great deal of stress.

I chose Midge's family to personify the Family Team Approach to household management even though my own family insists that it is the *only* family in America to function that way. But even if this were true, there is enough of value in knowing about it to share the information. After all, your family might be happy to accept the Family Team Approach!

Midge introduced me to all the concepts on how the family team works. Her family's current working schedule follows.

FAMILY TEAM SCHEDULE: MIDGE, JEFF, ANN

Chore	*Mon.*	*Tues.*	*Wed.*	*Thurs.*	*Fri.*	*Sat.*	*Sun.*	*Name*
Cooking	J	A	M	J	A	M	M	Jeff, Ann, Midge
Dishes	J	A	M	J	A	M	M	Jeff, Ann, Midge
Garbage	J	A	J	J	A	J	A	Jeff, Ann
Laundry		A	J					Ann, Jeff
Vacuum						J		Jeff
Bathrooms	A			A				Ann

JOB DESCRIPTION

Cooking:
- Make meal.
- Clean pots and put them in the dishwasher.
- Clean broiler when used.
- Clean counter top.

Dishes:
- After dinner, each person is responsible for clearing his or her own dishes.
- The person who cooks and cleans loads and empties the dishwasher after each meal. This has been found to decrease the mess.

Garbage:
- All garbage is to be placed in the utility room and neatly tied.
- Pails brought out and in on Monday and Thursday.

Laundry:
- Tuesday, each person brings laundry to utility room and separates whites from nonwhites. Colored clothes laundered.

- Wednesday, laundry day. All linens and towels washed.

Vacuum:
- Living area, kitchen.
- Individual bedroom left to person who occupies it.

Bathrooms:
- Wash tub, tile, toilet, and floor.
- Polish counters and mirrors.
- Put out clean towels

When things are going well, as they usually are, the family team functions in a terrific way. But lest you think the Brady Bunch is alive and well off the TV screen, let me tell you the Tale of the After Dinner Dish.

The Tale of the After Dinner Dish

Day 1, Sunday:

After a Sunday dinner of broiled steak, baked potatoes, and salad, everything was cleaned as normal by Jeff. Ann left her plate untouched on the table. P.S. Midge, who found it unpleasant, said nothing but pushed it to the side of the table.

Day 2, Monday:

All chores were done as normal. The plate now appears on the kitchen counter.

Day 3, Tuesday:

The plate seems to be growing "yucky." Signs of green mold appear. P.S. Midge says nothing but places a paper towel over it.

Day 4, Wednesday:

Midge is getting uncomfortable about the dish. A guest is coming for dinner, so she places the radio in front of the horrible, gooky green plate so the guest will not be upset.

Day 5, Thursday:

Midge finally speaks to each child separately. She expresses how uncomfortable the plate makes her feel. Midge: "I feel very uncomfortable with a green, gooky plate in the kitchen." She gets clear, logical arguments from both children. They explain:

Jeff: "Well, Ann didn't wash my laundry properly so. . . ."

Ann: "He was supposed to separate the laundry. . . ."

(I don't want to bore you, so I won't repeat the entire argument because you've heard it before. What is unique here is Midge's role.)

P.S. The plate remains untouched.

Day 6, Friday:

Midge announces to the two children that she is packing the car to leave. Because each person is going to visit friends for the weekend, Midge says: "We are leaving the house now, so the plate must be cleaned. You don't have time to fight about it any more."

P.S. When Midge returned, the dish was clean.

Moral: At no time did Midge

a. participate in the fight
b. manipulate the children
c. interfere with their chore
d. do the work herself

Of course, we all know that the Family Team Approach would be ideal if everyone contributed, but that doesn't always happen. How you handle members' lack of responsibility to the group determines the success of this approach. Midge avoided the no-win situation called "triangulation." Since most of us are familiar with the problems that occur when we step in the middle of two people having a problem, just avoiding triangulation is a plus for the Family Team Approach! The key to success in this approach is that once you give up a chore it no longer belongs to you. It cannot be done in your style, your terms, or at your convenience. In fact, you cannot do it. When it is not done properly you have to let it go. It might be uncomfortable occasionally, but, as Midge says, "This kind of thing happens very rarely. It will be a long time before this happens again. Even though I felt uncomfortable, the family team usually works and is really worth it."

How a Yachting Crew Divides Chores, or You Don't Have to Be Family to Work as a Team!

On a cold and stormy winter's night in 1984, I attended a lecture sponsored by our local cruising club because the guest speaker was Patience Wales of *Sail* magazine. I convinced myself that if she could sail in the Caribbean with an all-woman crew, I could manage to drive the few miles in the snow to hear her talk about it. Besides, I looked forward to meeting the female managing editor of a magazine with mostly male readership.

What I didn't expect to glean from the lecture is a clever way to divide housekeeping duties. As you may or may not know, on a boat females often perform chores based on purely traditional expectations. Whether this is because men expect it and women expect to do it or because women prefer those chores to the major responsibilities of yachting is a subject for future discussion. Most "boating people," however, have noticed that women often provision the boat, prepare the food, serve the drinks, and clean up just as they usually do at home. This is particularly obvious on a racing boat that often has a crew of five to ten and the only female is the (usually exquisite) cook. The point is that the coed crew described here works as a family team should. For twenty years they have used a nontraditional approach to chores that we can now learn about and perhaps even adapt fo use in our own homes.

HOW TO DIVIDE CHORES PAINLESSLY

1. List each chore on a 3 x 5 card. For example, "meals" and "laundry" are general categories that should be divided into specific chores, each with its own card as follows

Meals:	*Laundry:*
make breakfast	bring to washer
set table	wash
clean up table	dry
put food away	fold
wash breakfast dishes or load dishwasher	sort
dry and put away dishes or unload dishwasher	put away

2. Divide the cards into categories such as daily chores, weekly chores, seasonal maintenance, repairs, errands, and so on to avoid inequities. Under "seasonal maintenance," for instance, the yachting crew might include
   - polish teak (spring/fall)
   - scrub underside (spring/fall)
   - paint bottom (winter)

   Your own cards could similarly include:

   - polish wood paneling (winter)
   - scrub lawn furniture (spring/fall)
   - paint the trim (summer)
3. Sit in a group that includes all the people involved and deal out the cards as if you were playing a card game.
4. Each player accepts the cards he or she receives or rejects a card by trading with another. Those cards that are least likely to be accepted (it's hard to choose to do some tasks) can be placed face down and selected and then kept if no more trades will take place.

According to Patience Wales, the boat crew has used this card system for years, and the crew members have become proficient, over time, in the chores that belong to them. They even enjoy a sense of satisfaction once they learn to do a new chore well. Perhaps their formula will help you to divide your household chores more equitably. With family cooperation, this system can work well for the following reasons:

- A light and lively attitude, particularly while playing the card game, makes the chores seem less onerous.
- Individual choice helps create satisfaction.
- Follow-up on everyone's part (and this includes consistent expectations) is an absolute must in order for the chores to be done.

But let's face it—if someone, or everyone, does not want to participate, no game on earth will help. Then you have to look for the deep-rooted cause of the problem and how you feel about it and try to deal with those issues first before you can expect change.

When He Won't and the Children Don't

You've looked at all the options, examined the alternatives, eliminated, delegated, tried family meetings, and even attempted to draw cards and choose chores. You've read about getting cooperation from children, sitters, housekeepers, hired help, and friends. But have you noticed who is missing from each scenario?

That's right: it's the supportive equal partner sharing fully in the household chores and management. Some spouses do their share and more. And in some families everyone pitches in the way the sailing crew did. In a perfect world all husbands would know when the baby needs to be changed, when the laundry has to be done, and what to defrost for dinner. But the statistical evidence shows that their number is small. Besides, if you are reading this book it is likely that you are not getting the support around the house that you need.

So, if you have the problem that "he won't and they don't" (for in most cases it seems to be the husband who won't), particularly if his attitude undermines your efforts, here are some ideas for convincing your children that chores belong not only to you but also to them.

It's a fact of life; he doesn't participate because he won't. But you've also accepted the reality that you love him, and you're willing to pay the price (by doing the household chores with no help from him) because he's terrific. You can certainly live with him but *You Can't Do it All!* So what do you do?

- Stop complaining! You've decided to accept him because of all his other great qualities, so why aggravate yourself further?
- Try valiantly to rationalize his behavior to yourself and to your children: "Daddy was brought up to believe that housework belongs to the wife. This isn't fair, but it's what he believes. We have to accept his belief, but we don't have to agree with him."
- Announce to your children that you will accept his weakness in this regard but will not excuse theirs: "It is my duty to teach my children that housework belongs to the entire family; it should not be a burden that one member bears alone. Your cooperation is an absolute necessity for this household's well-being."
- Don't do their chores even when you feel you are in a no-win situation. Keep expecting. Deny services if you must, and eventually they'll turn around.
- Don't give up!

WORKBOOK PAGES STEP BY STEP TO YOUR OWN PERSONAL DECISION

Step One: Establish Priorities

Who Does What in Your House?

Spend a few minutes to complete this chart. If you feel angry, perhaps it's time to consider changes. If you feel lucky, perhaps it's time to count your blessings!

Job	*Name*	*Percent You Do*	*Hours Per Week Other person*	*You*
1. Plans meals				
2. Shops for food				
3. Cooks				
4. Serves meals				
5. Cleans kitchen				
6. Puts away edibles				
7. Washes and dries dishes				
8. Loads and unloads dishwasher				
9. Collects laundry, loads washing machine, puts clothes in dryer, folds and puts away clothes				
10. Sweeps				
11. Dusts				
12. Cleans windows and mirrors				
13. Vacuums				

Job	*Name*	*Percent You Do*	*Hours Per Week Other person*	*You*
14. Polishes				
15. Irons				
16. Picks up				
17. Defrosts freezer				
18. Neatens medicine cabinet				
19. Keeps tools, gardening utensils, and other items straight				
17. Baby-sits				
18. Repairs car				
19. Fixes appliances				
20. Changes light bulbs				
21. Tends pets				
22. Runs errands				
23. Makes appointments				
24. Scrubs				
25. Shops for family needs				
26. Buys presents				
27. Parks car				
28. Tends plants				
29. Makes beds				
30. Pays bills				

How Willing Are You to Change? If you've discovered that change is due, consider your willingness to live with some of these changes in an effort to reduce your workload.

1. Will your family be willing to adjust to catch-as-catch-can dinners?

2. Do you care if your child leaves home in an unmatched outfit or with unbrushed hair?

3. Are you willing to place trust and faith in others to eliminate some of your housework?

4. Are you willing to change your high standards to ease your workload?

 ____

 ____

5. Can you deal with disapproval from others when their needs are not met?

 ____

 ____

6. Will you take risk to try out a new idea and then adopt another style if it doesn't work?

 ____

 ____

Step Two: Consider Alternatives

Ideas to Substitute Services for Purchases

It is not unusual for people to have such deeply set patterns for doing household chores that even though they are working and finding it difficult to keep up the household, they don't consider substituting someone else's labor for their own. As has already been stated, this is as true of female physicians and other highly paid professionals as it is of the average wage earner. If you are busy earning a salary just to survive, you can't use these ideas yet. But you can consider them and work toward the goal of being able to use them.

Let's look at basic household labor costs in dollars. I'll use $5 an hour as a labor cost because it is a number I can easily multiply. And let's assume that each of your purchases costs $20.

Perhaps, instead of going out for a $20 meal at a modestly priced restaurant, you might consider eating at home so you can buy four hours of domestic help. Or you might consider doing the gardening yourself for a month to pay for items you purchase.

Whatever your choice, it doesn't hurt to make a list equating wages with goods and services. That way, when you find yourself saying, "It's OK to buy another purse/toy/book/record/shirt, but it's not OK to hire someone to clean the house," perhaps you'll be able to work out an equation that tells you it is OK to hire someone to ease your burden at home.

Use this page to set up your own exchange list, substituting the cost of goods, for the cost of local labor.

Consider your personal hourly wage. If you see that two hours of your work equals eight hours of domestic services, or if living without that extra pair of shoes will buy you a month of laundry service, you might be more willing to hire a helper.

What to substitute	so you can hire

Consider How Many of Your Actual Work Hours = Goods and Services You Can Purchase.

When my work day is absolutely the pits, I take a deep breath and play this survival game in my head. It helps my own precarious mental health, so I offer it to you. Here is my mathematical mind-saver:

1. I divide my yearly salary by the *actual* number of days worked, arriving at a number equal to earnings per day.

2. I divide that figure *(per day income)* by the *actual* number of hours worked. This is my hourly wage.
3. Then, I consider how many of those hours were intolerable. (Often, it is only a fraction of one hour.)
4. I promise myself a gift for that exact sum. (I always ignore deducting taxes.)
5. Before I talk myself out of it, I do it! Immediate gratification works best in these moments, although sometimes even making an appointment or promising a future delight works.
6. I avoid guilt by repeating: I deserve this! I deserve this! I deserve this!

Step Three: Is the Price Tag Worth It?

Alternatives	*Advantage*	*Price Tag*
Hire a housekeeper	Freedom from many chores	Financial burden Loss of privacy
Supermom	Approval Lessens friction in home	Physical fatigue Stress
Typical Salaried Mother	No financial burden	Physical fatigue Frustration Asking for help causes friction Anger and resentment
Administrator	Freedom from many chores	Ultimate responsibility

Family Team	Shared responsibility gives satisfaction	Loss of control
Dollars Earned for Service	Freedom from heavy cleaning chores	Financial burden

Step Four: Positive Effects

Supermom

Approval. Let's face it, if you are willing to do everything, other family members will approve.

Tradition. The traditional role of women is clearly experienced by other family members.

Nurturing. This family lifestyle provides a certain quality of nurturing.

Sense of value. Supermom generates a feeling of value and strength by her endurance. This energy may serve to enhance the value of the homemaker.

Harmony. Less friction and conflict is experienced by family members who are not involved in household management.

Typical Salaried Mother

Clarity. There is no confusion or debate about who runs the household. The Typical Salaried Mother is responsible, and other family members are helping to do a job that ultimately belongs to her.

Control. The Typical Salaried Mother can anticipate and then determine how the management of the household will flow. She is not necessarily dependent on the cooperaiton of other family members, although they feel rewarded when they are responsible for doing a good job.

Role models. The Typical Salaried Mother provides a clear, traditional female role model for her children. Usually the father in this family provides a clear picture of the traditional male role.

The Administrator

Efficiency. Using skills of executive management, the Administrator runs a very effective household.

Security. There is a prevailing feeling of security among family members who recognize that their household functions smoothly.

Crises. The Administrator is usually prepared to handle unexpected crises because she has an effective backup system.

Learning to Follow Directions. Children of the Administrator are trained early in life to follow directions.

Allowance. Children can learn a direct relationship between work well done and financial reward.

Family Team Approach

Pride. Family members feel a sense of value in their contribution to a working family team.

Self-reliance. Family members learn that they are able to function with a sense of independence. Interdependency is learned, rather than dependency.

Nonsexist child rearing. Responsibilities are shared and distributed based on abilities rather than gender.

Active parenting. Good relationships are established when the children are young. Sharing time and activities in making a household work establishes a bonding that may last a lifetime.

Mutual respect. The Family Team Approach develops mutuality and a healthy respect for individuality that reduces the negative effects of authoritarianism.

Decision-making skills. Children learn to be responsible for their own decisions as the natural and logical consequences of their acts.

Leisure. Shared work also affords shared leisure time, which has the potential of developing friendships among family members.

Step Five: Where I Stand

I believe that (choose one)

- Supermom
- Typical Salaried Mother
- Administrator
- Family Team Approach
- Hired help

is the best household management decision for me because it

- gives me approval
- lets me control the flow of the household
- provides my children with traditional role models
- is the most efficient
- gives my family a sense of security
- teaches the children self-reliance

- promotes nonsexist child rearing
- teaches children decision-making skills
- affords us all leisure time
- promotes family pride
- promotes active parenting

Step Six: Act

1. My current household management needs are:
   1. ______________________________
   2. ______________________________
   3. ______________________________
   4. ______________________________
   5. ______________________________
2. These are changes I will make in household management so that I can start meeting these needs:
   1. ______________________________
   2. ______________________________
   3. ______________________________
   4. ______________________________
   5. ______________________________
3. These are possible reactions from family members of my family to each change.
   1. ______________________________
   2. ______________________________
   3. ______________________________
   4. ______________________________
   5. ______________________________
4. I am prepared to hear the following:
   1. "The other mothers. . . ."
   2. "When we were first married. . . ."
   3. "When I grow up/have kids, I will/won't. . . ."
   4. "A good mother should. . . ."
   5. "If you really loved me. . . ."

5. I am prepared to say the following:
   1. "You must be disappointed that . . . ."
   2. "It sounds like you feel hurt that. . . ."
   3. "Things are different now that. . . ."
   4. "It takes time to get comfortable with new ways. . . ."

6. I am prepared to feel
   1. Self-doubt
   2. Anxiety
   3. Anger
   4. Hurt

7. I am prepared to remind myself that
   1. The old ways cannot work here anymore.
   2. You are in a new place and need to work through new ways.

Now that you have decided what style of household management suits you, you are ready. Unless you have determined that you feel best doing everything for everyone, the following examples offer you a variety of rosters to help you communicate and to define chores and expectations for those who will help you. These rosters are particularly handy if you are hiring helpers for the first time and don't know what to ask or what reasonably to expect.

Communication between worker and employee is very important. Naturally, you have to interview and discuss (even if it feels as though you are playing charades when your helper doesn't speak the language) the specific chores you expect. Saying, "Do this," and handing someone a list doesn't make for good employer/employee relations. But discussing what needs to be done, what the other person is willing or not willing to do, and then offering to write out the terms so the person will have them for reference will help. I always make many copies of these lists so I have them available whenever a newcomer starts working or whenever I feel a list will remind the worker to do certain chores.

The suggested ways of organizing work can't, of course, change already established behavior. *You* have to do that. But they *will* help you communicate expectations clearly.

Once-a-Week Help

A conversation with the working wife of a very active husband reminded me that you don't need to have children to have the myriad managerial problems of running a household. (In fact, children can be the best helpers and, as we know some adults can be the worst ones!) She recently hired a weekly cleaning person but finds that she is so unused to giving orders that she doesn't know what to ask her employee to do. The cleaning woman doesn't speak English, and the only words she was able to repeat were "clean and dust." It's not surprising that my friend feels she isn't getting her money's worth, nor is it unusual to hear her husband tease her by saying things like "By the time you spend two hours straightening the house and putting things away, another hour doing the laundry and making and serving her lunch, you might as well clean yourself." Moreover, they both resented having their private time on Saturdays interrupted by the stranger.

Well, my friend is not so very different from any of us when we first hire help. This is especially true for those of us, like her, who were brought up watching our mothers serve, who were taught to serve our fathers and guests, and who married men who expected us to serve them.

Learning how to have others help us is certainly worth the investment even if it does take a little time to decide the specific tasks that need to be done and to make up lists to suit your own household.

Once having determined that she didn't want to work around the house with her helper (some people prefer to work in tandem and get everything done at once), I made some suggestions for her, which I'll share with you.

- Provide food, not restaurant service.
- Ask the helper to start each work day by stripping beds and adding bathroom towels for first load of laundry.
- Make a list of chores to be done every week and an additional list of different half-hour or hour tasks to be done each week.
- Divide tasks into small, easy-to-complete segments. This system works as well for hired help as it does for children.
- Get out of the way. If your are trusting, leave the premises. Otherwise, stay in another room. Few people do their best work when they are watched and interrupted.
- If the person isn't familiar with cleaning products and you are particular about what you want used, show it to them.
- I have often hired help who preferred specific products and who purchased them for me. I laid out the money and they bought the products and gave me the receipt.

ONCE-A-WEEK CLEANING ROSTER:*

MASTER BEDROOM

Strip bed and gather towels for laundry
Vacuum (check for cobwebs)
Dust and polish furniture
Clean mirror
Make bed

LIVING/DINING ROOM

Dust and polish
Vacuum
  Pick up any dead leaves from plants
  Move couch
  Check for cobwebs
Use window cleaner on glass tables

KITCHEN

Damp-mop floor
Use stainless steel cleanser on sink

*Do not enter children's rooms unless specifically requested.

Wipe cabinets and appliances
Clean toaster and microwave inside

DO ONE OF THESE EACH WEEK:
Clean inside of oven or refrigerator
Seal butcher block (mineral oil) or floor tiles (sealer)

DEN
Damp-mop
Dust (avoid desk top unless clear)

OFFICE/GUEST ROOM
Damp-mop (Clear detergent ammonia)
DO NOT TOUCH DESK!!!
Launder sheets/make bed when undone

BATHROOMS
Spray/scrub/do tile monthly

LAUNDRY ROOM
Damp-mop
Neaten please!!!
Clean machines

USE ONE HOUR EACH WEEK FOR OCCASIONAL CHORES
PLEASE WRITE DATE NEXT TO THE CHORE YOU'VE DONE

_______ Medicine cabinet shelves
_______ Floors of closets (vacuum and dust)
_______ Wipe around doors and walls
_______ Clean under the kitchen sink
_______ Vacuum, dust, and tidy bedroom with request on door
_______ Clean and arrange shelf in pantry
_______ Move books and dust a book shelf

_______ Laundry room closet (tidy; mop floor)
_______ Polish marble table in den
_______ Polish stainless on stools and chair in living room
_______ Neaten linen closet
_______ Wipe kitchen cabinets
_______ Clean glass on front doors and/or window
_______ Remove and wash light fixtures

Daily Help

If you are lucky enough to have daily housekeeping help, it is a good idea to provide clear, written instructions. I used this plan when I had live-in help before Jenifer started nursery school. Alison and Sharon were about seven and ten and did their own laundry and were supposed to tidy their rooms. In those days Bob still expected his laundry done for him. (Those days are gone forever!)

Daily Chores	*Persons(s) Responsible*
Load and empty dishwasher	_______
Empty trash	_______
Wipe table and counters	_______
Do wash, dry, fold, put away	_______
Sweep or damp-mop kitchen floor	_______
Make master bedroom bed	_______
Straighten den (empty ashtrays)	_______
Take garbage pails out and in Mon.–Thurs.	_______
Clean top of stove and toaster	_______
Wipe surfaces in bathrooms	_______
Set dinner table	_______

Weekly Chores

Monday:

Vacuum, dust, mop downstairs

Wipe leather couch, dust pictures, water plants, wipe window sills, check for cobwebs, clean mirrors with glass cleaner.

Do Bob's laundry and/or Jenifer's

Tuesday:

Jenifer's bedroom (notice that the older sisters were responsible for their own rooms)

- Strip bed, wash sheets, return to bed
- Sweep under bed, damp-mop floor
- Do shelves if possible
- Do her laundry after sheets

Wednesday:

Master bedroom and bath

- Wash, dry, and return sheets and towels
- Vacuum and dust room and shelves (top of chest)
- Clean all mirrors and bathroom glass with glass cleaner
- Arrange makeup table if possible

Thursday:

Children's bath and rooms

- Tub, tile, toilet, floors, and sink
- Wash all towels and return
- Vacuum children's rooms IF they are tidy

Friday:

Do downstairs cleaning again and catch-up day

OCCASIONAL JOBS WHEN THERE IS EXTRA TIME OR PER REQUEST AS NEEDED

_____	refrigerator	_____	linen closet
_____	silver	_____	pantry closet
_____	ironing	_____	windows (one room each week)
_____	stove	_____	polish machines
_____	polish cabinets	_____	hand wash

This list is very, very old, and our household has had many changes over the years. Since then, I've packed up the silver. Laundry is done by whoever wears it now, and they iron for themselves! Windows are done by a window washer, and I bought a self-cleaning oven. With grown-up children, and only one teenager living at home, I neither need nor want the daily help that made it possible for me to work with three little ones. Now, we have once-a-week household help.

Hiring a Cleaning Service

I'll never forget the first time I hired a cleaning service. At that time, I had a daily sitter who arrived at 6:00 A.M. and got Jenifer off to school by 9:00 A.M. We couldn't afford help for more than fifteen hours a week, plus some afternoon or evening baby-sitting. Although my sitter was like a Cinderella in performing little chores (she unloaded the dishwasher, did the laundry, made the coffee, even drove my husband to the railroad station), she was not expected to scrub the floors or search for cobwebs. Those tasks were definitely not in her job description.

Through a wonderfully ironic twist of fate, my copy of *Ms.* magazine arrived at about the same time as the three cleaning men. There sat I, on the reclining chair I had bought my husband for his birthday, reading the latest news from the feminist front, while three professionals scrubbed, polished, and waxed the floors. What a luxury! What a day!

If you handle such routine houshold chores as shopping, cooking, dishes, and laundry, but need professionals to do the heavy work, consider hiring a cleaning service. These services prefer weekly or bimonthly clients, but I have used them annually, seasonally, before parties, or whenever the looks of the house makes me holler "HELP!"

THESE JOBS CAN BE DELEGATED TO A CLEANING SERVICE

- They do ceilings, walls, doors, and floors.
- They scrub and wax floors with professional equipment.

- They scrub and polish tubs, tiles, and toilets.
- They polish wood paneling and kitchen cabinets.
- They do mirrors.
- They vacuum and turn mattresses (they prefer them stripped).

THERE MIGHT BE AN EXTRA CHARGE FOR THESE JOBS

- Interior of refrigerators. (This is personal, and they prefer not to do it.)
- Interior of oven.
- Windows.
- Rug cleaning.

THESE CHORES ARE NOT USUALLY DONE BY CLEANING SERVICES

- Laundry
- Dishes
- Making the beds

SUGGESTIONS

- Comparison shop by phone.
- Get references.
- Try to have someone at home the first time, at least.
- Make sure the service is bonded and insured.

Step Seven: Reevaluation

I will reevaluate my household management decision in _______ weeks/months/semester/duration of job span.

If noticeable changes take place or when something stops working I will:

STOP

ASK WHY?

1. Why isn't it working?
2. Why am I not content?

3. Why is my family miserable?

MAKE CHANGES

1. What can we do to make it more comfortable?
2. What jobs can we eliminate or delegate?
3. What can we do to get people to meet their responsibilities?

TRY ANOTHER ALTERNATIVE

1. There are no simple solutions, only intelligent choices.

TRANSPORTATION

THE transportation years, from the time you carry your first baby to the sitter's house until your youngest offspring learns to drive, present myriad problems for the working mother. Determining transportation needs and finding viable solutions require searching questions and careful planning. Each year, and often each season, as your children grow, new complications arise.

People who are fortunate enough to live near available and economical mass transportation have fewer problems, but they do have to worry about safety, so they often have to hire a person to accompany the children to their activities during the preteen years. This section offers valuable insights for those parents.

If you are career woman planning to live in the suburbs and continue your career while raising your children, this section is for you. If you are already hassled with the transportation problems of the typical suburban mother, and you are planning to become a Typical Salaried Mother, then commit this material to memory!

The world has changed. For many women, the dream of a

house in the suburbs preceded the desire to enter the marketplace. Transportation convenience was rarely a criterion in our initial choice of a place to live. I think the hidden assumption in both the suburban developers' and the suburban buyers' minds was pretty much the same:

Each house will have two cars. One of those cars (his) will be gone all day. The other car (yours) has a chauffeur sitting in it, smiling and ready. Guess who?

But the world has changed. Today, so many mothers are working that it is an obstacle just to find an at-home mother who is available as a contact to name on the emergency card children are required to have for the school nurse, not to mention the backup system necessary for real emergencies.

What has not changed in suburbia is the appalling lack of public transportation. Therefore, we have to figure out the easiest and most efficient way to get our kids everywhere. When we are unavailable, our little problem often escalates to one of gargantuan aggravation. Let's read how some mothers manage.

ROLE MODELS

My Mother the Car: KAY

Kay is a working mother, married to a man who truly believes that transporting the children, like tending the household, is a responsibility that belongs to his wife.

When Kay's growing family chose to leave their city apartment to buy a house in the suburbs, Kay understood that she would be faced with a longer work day as a commuter and the problems of transporting herself and her children.

Nevertheless, Kay chose to do all the driving herself.

Kay is a buyer of housewares by profession. Although she works for a chain of department stores, her hours are regular. Occasionally she travels to trade shows, but ordinarily the dealers come to her office, by appointment, to show their wares. Each day, Kay leaves her office promptly at five to rush home and begin her driving schedule. She looks forward to the half-hour drive home as a time to unwind and get ready for the kids. Then she spends the next half hour in uninterrupted one-to-one parenting. For Kay, the time spent taking her children to their lessons and back is the most precious time they spend together. It's intimate and theirs alone.

QUESTIONS

1. Do you share Kay's attitude toward driving the children?

2. Can you manage the schedule after work?

3. Is personally driving the children *your* priority as it is Kay's?

4. Do you have a backup driver available?

5. Is Kay overcompensating or fulfilling her role?

Your Mother the Car Isn't Available: IRVINA

In California and Florida teenagers are licensed drivers at age fifteen. In New York State, one hears the possibility of raising the driving age to eighteen. Working mothers unite! I, who wake up every morning in the driving position, could organize a campaign to lower the legal age limit. I'm sure there are working mothers who would be willing to give their responsible fifteen-year-olds the car to free themselves from the wheel.

My daughter, the swimmer, is a typical example of the child who needed a chauffeur. By the time Sharon was ten, in 1972, she had determined to swim in the 1980 Olympics. To her credit, at the age of fifteen, she was still swimming and I was still driving. But by then we also argued a lot.

Sharon's swimming schedule, at a pool located seven miles away, was as follows:

Monday–Friday	5 P.M.–7 P.M.
Saturday	8 A.M.–11 A.M.
Summers (seven days)	6 A.M.–8 A.M.
Sunday	Meets: here, there, and everywhere

Sharon also had clear-cut definitions of the role of the "real mother." In addition to her work and household responsibilities, and while fitting in the needs of the family, the "real mother" would:

- Provide transportation (preferably individualized)
- Watch all practices (lap after lap)
- Buy all equipment (necessary and desired)
- Root for her (here, there, and everywhere)
- Make all necessary adjustments such as dropping religious school, changing the dinner hour, and finding alternate transportation for her husband.
- Provide the emotional support she deserved.

In retrospect, I realize that our problem was a simple one of perception. I felt I was supportive, but Sharon felt that I didn't care! If I had to live those years again, I think I would act more interested—ask more questions and appear more genuinely enthusiastic.

I, on the other hand, felt it was my parental obligation to

- Support her interest with enthusiasm (I even joined the parent group)
- Provide transportation (but not necessarily drive myself)
- Buy all necessary equipment (key word: necessary)
- Root for her at meets whenever possible

The differences in our expectations do not appear to be enormous. But even little differences can escalate into major conflicts. Sharon felt that if I were a "real mother," I would watch every practice session. I, on the other hand, had neither the time nor the inclination to watch her swim lap after lap every day.

Nevertheless, there were other mothers who were there every afternoon. They knew every child, knew everything the coach was doing, knew how well or not the coaches and swimmers did their jobs. They arranged their daily lives to be there for their swimmers. Some even told the coach what to do and how to do it better. Others held the towels for their teenaged children. They dried their bodies and even cleaned their ears. My children informed me that "real mothers" did those things willingly.

Perhaps I didn't win the "real mother" award from my swimmer. But I had been notified by my employer either to complete certification, in a new subject area, or to look for a job elsewhere. Some decisions can be made in two seconds: I enrolled in graduate school once again. Of course, it almost goes without saying that the classes met four afternoons a week, during the same hours that Sharon swam laps.

Hire a Driver

Our alternatives were easy to spot:

1. Sharon could retire from swimming
2. I could hire a driver

Naturally, I placed an ad in the newspaper the day I registered for school, and we hired the driver that week. She was wonderful! So was her unemployed husband, who often helped out. She did errands en route, drove Sharon to and fro, and, when able, raced home, folded laundry, and even prepared dinner. Often, he would drive Sharon while she helped around the house. Two for the price of one! Even though the cost of a driver meant eliminating a cleaning person once a week, it was money well spent. Our lives became more manageable, and no one seemed to mind cleaning together on Saturdays.

Since then, I've often hired drivers. Commuting college students need gas money and, if their schedule coincides with your needs, they can be extremely helpful. Retired people, who have few responsibilities and often more strength than you can imagine, make wonderful drivers. Again, it is frequently less aggravating to delegate the chore and pay someone else to do it than to be burdened with the job yourself. Trade-offs might just be worthwhile.

QUESTIONS:

	Yes	No
1. Are you able/willing to pay someone to provide transportation?	____	____
2. Can you make the financial trade-offs?	____	____
3. Can you barter for these services?	____	____
4. Would your children understand even if the decision were *not* based on need?	____	____
5. Once you make the decision to hire, can you relinquish the responsibility?	____	____

NOTE: ONCE THE DECISION IS MADE TO FIND A DRIVING SUBSTITUTE, THE SUBJECT IS NO LONGER NEGOTIABLE. YOU ARE FREE!

Car Pools

Station wagons and car pools are as synonymous with suburbia as Little League and lawn mowers. There was a period in my life when the ultimate symbol of luxurious living was that little button that lowered the back window. Not to get out in the rain! Not to open the back door four times an evening! It was my personal daydream to be able to buy a car with that little button.

How, you might ask, did a person who gave such careful thought to transportation end up spending her life in a car pool? Frankly, it was because I tried to be a good mother. But when my children reached the age when their religious education required my transporting them to our synagogue two days a week after school, and sometimes on Friday night or Saturday morning and Sunday, I realized that I could not do it all and joined a car pool.

Where, you might wonder, was my loving spouse during these driving years? He traveled! No matter what his schedule, it never seemed to fit in with the children's. It did, however, suit the washing machine perfectly. He would fly away, and the washing machine would overflow. Like clockwork, it adapted to his schedule.

Nevertheless, those car pool years remain in the forefront of my memory. One afternoon, I realized that anyone seen driving in a station wagon fit a specific life pattern. The wagon said it all! It became crystal clear on the day I did not drive my station wagon.

I was driving to the city, in my husband's new toy, a ten-year-old newly rebuilt Alfa Romeo. Three men paid attention to me on the expressway: One honked, then grinned. The second drove alongside and shoved a cardboard sign in the window, upon which was scrawled, "You're cute!" The third paid my fare through the Midtown tunnel.

Now, this was no ordinary situation. I checked the mirror to see if I had transformed into an exotic beauty. Not by a long shot! I hadn't changed a bit! The difference was in the perception of the people who fantasize while driving: a redhead alone in a sports car is automatically exciting, sexy, and available! Anyway, that was the day I realized that my wagon announced my status in life: chauffeur, mother, errand doer—the wagon says it all.

No, I didn't run out and sell the wagon. We used it for years to transport scouts to meetings, sailors to boats, campers to camp, and cousins to the beach. The car pool gave that wagon character with a patina of smudge. And sometimes now, when I see another family wagon, I miss it and the life it represents.

The Car Pool Champion: CAROLINE

Caroline, with whom I shared the religious school car pool, was a true champion. Her car pool lists and charts adorned her kitchen office wall in a way that would rival any candidate's campaign headquarters. Caroline was an active working mother whose three children had equally busy schedules. As is often the case, the busiest person, the one with the least available time, ends up coordinating and organizing so as to obtain maximum efficiency for herself. Thus Caroline did all the negotiating, planning, scheduling, telephoning, and typing for her various car pools.

Promptness and reliability were important factors in choosing the drivers. Caroline had it all down to a science. Her schedule was rigid. She drove after her work day and on Sunday mornings. She was never late. She never forgot a passenger. She hired backup drivers on occasion. She never called to cancel. And she was very unhappy if any other driver wasn't equally up to snuff.

On the wall, in the part of the kitchen I refer to as the control center (near the phone, bulletin board, and grocery lists), were her car pool paraphernalia:

TYPED LISTS OF CAR POOL PERSONNEL

Name Parent's Name Address/Directions Telephone #

SEPARATE LISTS OF EACH CAR POOL

1. *Destination*
2. *Arrival time*
3. *Departure Time*
4. *Directions*

COLOR CODING FOR EACH CHILD
1. *Blue for Betty*
2. *Green for Jeff*
3. *Red for Sandy*

LETTER LABELS ON EACH LIST
A. *Soccer*
B. *Religious school*
C. *Scouts*

ONE ENORMOUS CALENDAR
All information gathered into weekly and monthly schedules.

Car Pool Pitfalls

The car pool is known to be efficient and economical and to save millions of people hours. But take a look at the following scenarios before you get involved. The drawbacks in terms of aggravation and stress must be considered.

SCENARIO #1

You are tired from a typical, nonstressful day at work. You rush home knowing that you have to drive your Little Lovely to Little League.

You run in the door, kiss the others, say hello, and throw something in the oven. L.L. is ready, bat and glove in hand, hat firmly planted on pony tail.

With L.L. in the back seat, you start the car and race around the corner, in the opposite direction from the playing field, stop, honk the horn, and wait. Then you find out that either:

a. No one is home (no phone call)
b. The player is ill (no phone call)
c. The dawdler isn't ready (again!)

Sure, it's a minor aggravation, but try it four times a week for a while and frustration sets in, which soon turns to anger directed at the perfectly innocent child (yours) seated behind you.

SCENARIO #2

Your child is sick. You wish that you could rush home, sit by the bedside, make chicken soup, and give some TLC. But you can't! Why not? Because today is your day to drive the other children to scouts. You know that they depend on you. Besides, it is easier to disappoint your own love than to make the time to make the phone calls to cancel. You know that if you cancel you might as well forget expecting the other parents ever to drive your child again!

SCENARIO #3

The phone rings at 7:10 A.M. Someone announces that your child must attend an extra afternoon practice. You remind the someone that surely he could have called yesterday when it *might* have been possible to make the necessary arrangements. You are reminded that *you* are in charge of the car pool and hear the phone slam. Great, huh?

SCENARIO #4

You went to work to be independent.

You wanted to control your own destiny.

Now you find yourself controlled by people who care nothing for promptness, reliability, or even common courtesy.

MORAL:
WEIGH THE CAR POOL CAREFULLY. THE DOLLAR SAVINGS MIGHT NOT BE WORTH THE PRICE YOU PAY!!!

Let's look at what other mothers do.

Dial-a-Ride: LOUISE

Louise is an executive with a large New York City corportion. Her office hours are from nine to five. She leaves her suburban home about seven in the morning returns twelve hours later to begin her family time. As a commuter, she has no time to drive her children to their activities. And if you have ever commuted, you know that she has no strength, either.

I met Louise when she had her house up for sale. It fulfilled my every dream, and after walking through it we sat down to discuss the cold, hard, and disillusioning data:

When she told me the price, I said "reasonable."

When she told me what the upkeep cost, I said "minimal."

When she told me what it cost to heat, I said "normal."

When she told me what the electricity bill was, I said "average."

But when she told me about the taxis, I said "What?!?"

"Oh! yes," she replied, "every child has an account with Dial-a-Ride. Town and schools are too far away, and now all the car pool mothers work. Dial-a-Ride takes wonderful care of the children. They even know them by name!"

Taxis seemed elitist to me, and our budget included no dollars for them, so our conversation ended.

I think often about Louise, now, because I always leave emergency money in the jar for a taxi!

QUESTIONS:

	Yes	No
1. Will taxi service solve your transportation needs?	____	____
2. Will your child be willing to go by cab when necessary?	____	____
3. Can you pay the high cost of this service?	____	____

4. Will your child appreciate the ride or accuse you of not doing your job? ____ ____

Children of Mothers Who Don't Drive Survive: JOANNE

Some of us know children of mothers who don't drive. These kids don't ask their mothers for rides because they know the answer in advance. Children ask only for what they

a. expect
b. hope for
c. can negotiate

JoAnne, a former neighbor of mine drove. She drove to work, to the doctor's, to shop, and each week she drove the blind on their errands. But she did not drive her children—she didn't believe in it!

JoAnne was what my children described as a "real mother." She sewed clothes, baked cookies, popped popcorn to decorate the Christmas tree, and all the rest. She was the teacher/director of a local nursery school by day and a perpetual student by night, always increasing her credentials. I really admired her!

Her husband traveled back and forth from Peru for business, so JoAnne was in charge of running the household. Daddy came home like a visiting uncle and could hardly be expected to take care of the details. JoAnne's philosophy helped her through some trying years. She strongly believed that the school offered enough activities for any normal child and therefore never offered to spend money on lessons for anyone.

Need I mention that all of her children were genius students, active in all school and church affairs? They learned to skate when the ice froze on the lake (not by being driven to the rink), they swam when Red Cross was at the local beach (JoAnne never drove to a pool), and they did everything better than everyone else.

So it's impossible to know what's best. Kay may be driving, Caroline may be coordinating, and I may be paying through the nose while JoAnne is sitting somewhere in Lima, Peru, smiling knowingly because ultimately, *we all do what we want to do.*

WORKBOOK PAGES STEP BY STEP TO YOUR OWN PERSONAL DECISION

Step One: Establish Priorities

Whether you are already a working women or contemplating going to work, you must make certain decisions regarding your availability to provide transportation.

	YES	NO
1. Is it absolutely necessary that you be available to drive?	____	____
2. Are you unavailable to transport everybody?	____	____
3. Are you willing to delegate driving to someone else, even if it means paying for the service?	____	____
4. Do you suffer guilt when you say, "No, I can't drive?"	____	____
5. Are you willing to curtail your children's activities to cut down on transportation needs?	____	____
6. Do you have an available support system (husband, mother, relative, friend, neighbor) to share the transportation responsibilities?	____	____

7. Are you willing to adjust your work to meet your transportation responsibilities?	____	____
8. Do you have a reliable backup system?	____	____
9. When you are unavailable, do you suffer loss of approval from:		
your mate?	____	____
your children?	____	____
other people?	____	____
10. Do you use transportation as a means of expressing your love?	____	____
11. Does your family recognize that your needs are as important as their own?	____	____
12. Is their approval more important than your need to work?	____	____
13. Are your children willing to walk, ride bikes, or go with a friend if possible?	____	____
14. Is driving time stressful for you?	____	____
15. Do family members perceive transportation as your responsibility or a mutual one?	____	____

Insist upon Safety as a Priority

1. Make sure your children know safety rules and regulations.
2. Check out all equipment:
   a. Bikes must have good brakes and reflectors.
   b. Check out the cars in the car pool or taxi company, too.
3. Clothing is important:
   a. If you buy bright orange or yellow jackets you can

eliminate the fear that your walking or biking child will not be seen in the dusk. It's a lot easier than asking them to wear vests because they won't do it.

4. Make time for trial runs: teach your child, even when accompanied, to walk on certain streets or on a particular side of the street. When safety is the main concern, you must consider each detail.

Step Two: Consider Alternatives

Alternative #1: Eliminate Whenever Possible

1. Encourage activities:
   a. in school
   b. in the neighborhood
   c. at home

   It could be easier for you to arrange a dancing class nearby than to transport your child to a weekly class.
2. Make transportation a criterion for selection:
   a. Can Johnny walk to guitar lessons?
   b. Hire a tutor who comes to the house.
   c. Help your child find a job in the neighborhood (after school responsibility is very important to keep children productive and out of trouble).
3. Learn to distinguish your child's casual wants from true needs:
   a. Feel out your child's enthusiasm.
   b. This good test is almost foolproof: Is the child willing to pay for it in time, energy, responsibility, or money?
4. Prioritize: Each person is allowed one activity per year.

Alternative #2: Make Convenience One Criterion for Choosing a Place to Live

Perhaps you aren't moving in the near future, but if you are, think about convenience. I knew all about the transportation problems when we bought our second house in 1968. Not having enough money for two cars, I was, for a very long school year, dependent on someone to drive me to work. We had to organize our time just to be able to use the car for a trip to the grocery store. As a working mother expecting our third child, I gave transportation convenience priority importance. We chose a house within walking or biking distance of the following locations:

Place	*Rationale*
Train	My husband commutes.
Bus	Sitters might need it.
Schools	I leave early, and they might stay late.
Library	I hoped the children would read a lot.
Grocery store	We might run out of milk.
Cleaners	He might run out of shirts.
Bank	We always run out of money.
Stores	Notebooks and jeans could be purchased by the kids.
Medical buildings	Older children could go for checkups on their own.
Entertainment	Movies, bowling, and beach all within reach.

Let's score my success quotient:

Score 10 for full use
Score 5 for partial use
Score 3 for backups and emergencies

Place	*Use*	*Score*
Train	He walks if I can't meet him.	5
Bus	Suburban kids reject the bus!	3
Schools	They walked or rode to games, too.	10
Library	They could take out and return books and do research alone.	10
Grocery	The nearest burned down.	5
Cleaners	They don't do shirts very well.	5
Bank	It's there, and I use it.	10
Stores	This was terrific. They chose their own purchases!	10
Medical building	I go to hold hands; they go alone if I'm not available	5
Entertainment	Movies, bowling, and beach are all within reach.	10
		73

Look at my score (and I was trying).

Make a list of your top ten transportation needs and score according to whether or not your children walk/bike on their own.

Score 10	Always
Score 5	Usually
Score 3	Sometimes
Score 0	Never

Place	*Use*	*Score*
1.		
2.		
3.		
4.		
5.		
6.		
7.		

8. ____________________
9. ____________________
10. ____________________

TOTAL: __

How often does your family walk or bike? I am going to assume that you didn't do much better than I. You probably didn't use transportation as a criterion when selecting your home either. Most of us don't when we first look for an affordable place to live with a kitchen that works and enough bedrooms. Now, what we have to do is plan these inconvenient transportation needs according to our limited availability.

Alternative #3: Determine Your Own Availability

1. Don't fool around. If you cannot do one more thing, say so.
2. Clearly define what you are willing to contribute and stick to it.
3. Do not assume a responsibility you cannot fulfill.
4. When you say "no," do so without guilt or lectures. Do you think every mother who doesn't drive feels guilty about it?
5. If you choose to make time and energy available, don't blame your children and dump guilt on them because you're tired. Remember, you chose to do it.

Alternative #4:Consider Attitudes

1. What are your expectations from your children?
   a. Are they ready?
   b. Are they prepared?

c. Do they meet their other obligations?
d. Do they give you consideration?
e. What is their attitude when they ask to be taken somewhere?
f. Do they attempt to plan their activities around your availability?

2. What are their expectations?
   a. Are you a "real mother" or a chauffeur?
   b. Are their expectations reasonable?
   c. Can you meet them?
   d. Is it a priority to your child that you personally chauffeur?

Alternative #5: Who Goes Where? Who Drives or Transports in Your Family?

Fill in the following chart and then circle whatever portion of the transportation obligations you fulfill. This will give you a clear picture of whether your transportation chores are fairly distributed. Perhaps if you show the completed page to your children or spouse, they will realize that some changes are needed. It worked for me—maybe it will work for you.

People Who Need to be Transported

Destinations
1. ______________________________
2. ______________________________
3. ______________________________
4. ______________________________
5. ______________________________
6. ______________________________
7. ______________________________

8. ____________________
9. ____________________
10. ____________________

TOTAL: __

Step Three: Is the Price Tag Worth It?

Alternatives	*Price Tag*
Walk/bike	Best bet
Car pool	Try it, but be careful
Barter services	Oldie but goodie (the kids could mow a lawn)
Hire a driver	Minimum wage plus gas money
Taxi	Luxury price but worthwhile
Hitchhike	Not recommended, but it must be discussed

I must add a word about hitchhiking. As a parent and teacher I've never approved of or heard anyone recommend hitchhiking to anyone. It is dangerous, and it can be deadly. Nevertheless, kids do it every day. Talk to your preteenage children about the safest ways to hitchhike. (This is like talking about alcohol, pot, or sex.) You say: I know *you* would never do it, but in case you have friends who do, they should

- Always choose the car and driver. This is simple if you stand at a well-lit, busy place like McDonald's, a gas station, or shopping center.
- *Never* stand or walk on the side of the road because there you are vulnerable. Once a car pulls to a stop, a hitchhiker is in a very precarious position alone on the side of a road.
- Get in a car only if it is occupied by children. Mothers or fathers driving with their children are unlikely to rape or murder teenagers.

- Make a sign and roll it up and carry it. Stand in the parking lot of a school, beach, or shopping center and let the driver know where you want to go.

The major price tag of working mothers' experience is called "loss of approval." Women who are ready to move or who have moved into the marketplace should ask themselves one major question: Am I ready to move in a direction that seeks self-approval (as a support system) rather than the approval of others? This question is more pressing for the woman who is choosing to work for reasons that do not include economic necessity. The woman who works to meet the economic needs of her family does not risk disapproval. The one who comes from a happy marriage in which the husband earns a living, however, risks a great deal of disapproval from her children, her spouse, her nonworking friends, and particularly her own relations.

The price of your transportation decisions far exceeds the dollars spent to hire a driver. No matter what form of transportation you choose, it is wise to accept the consequences of your decision in advance. Being aware of the price tag might help you deal with those consequences most effectively, thereby decreasing the amount of guilt attached.

Loss of approval. If your family has grown up used to having you as the all-purpose and available chauffeur, you will probably be understanding when your children say, "Before you went to work, you picked me up when it was raining" or "Jane's mother [who doesn't work] takes her shopping after school" or "Oh, I forgot you're busy."

Before you make your career decision ask yourself: Am I ready to move in a direction that seeks self-approval (as a support system) rather than the approval of others?

Investment of time. Transportation alternatives might require you to spend time with people you choose to be with only because you need them to drive. You may need to invest time establishing a working relationship with car pool associates or a neighbor, making a barter arrangement, or even spend additional work time to pay for driving services.

Guilt. A part of the transportation problem is somewhat superficial and can be conquered by using a combination of the alternatives mentioned above. It is the underlying problem that must be resolved for the working mother—the basic conflict that is referred to as the role of the real mother versus the non-caring one. Some women are willing to be totally available to fulfill their children's needs, other mothers are manipulated by their children to fulfill their every whim, and the working mother often succumbs because of her own feelings of guilt. Guilt will be dealt with as a separate issue, but it is very important for you to understand why and what you are doing.

- Are you driving to show your child love?
- Do your children understand why you need to work outside of the home?
- Do your children expect you to be available even though you have an enormously difficult time in so doing?
- Do you drop everything, leave meetings, and rush home to drive?
- Do you ever feel that you'd rather be working or doing something to please yourself when you are busy pleasing other people?
- Once the arrangements have been made for someone else to take over, can you remove yourself from the issue, free yourself from concern over it?
- Once you have determined that your child can go safely alone, do you remain in control by issuing constant reminders? Can you give the child the trust that encourages confidence and independence?

It cannot be stressed enough that children whose parents do not drive survive; children whose parents do not choose to take them substitute activities that can be equally valuable. Drop your guilt!

I'm really trying on this one. If you recall my initial list of the top ten places family members need to go, I omitted house of worship. As a direct result, I was involved in a car pool (which I found constrictive), and I ended up resenting that I had to argue with my children to get them to attend while at the same time I was being inconvenienced. Consequently, I neglected the religious education of my youngest, who might well grow up a heathen. Do I feel guilt? YOU BET! Did I want to drive? NOT A BIT!

Conflicts. How do you handle the following problems?

- Do you have a reliable backup system?
- Does the family, as a group, suffer because of one person's schedule?
- When "who's" on first and "what's" on second and you are late at the office, "what happens?"
- Is the time spent driving together quality time or craziness?

Effect on others: Whatever alternative transportation decision you have made, do not dwell on the guilt that mothers share because they feel they have deprived their children. Remember "to drive" is not synonymous with "to love." You can feel reassured that your transportation decision has offered your children some of the following growth experiences:

- Learning to be on time
- Taking responsibility for belongings
- Recognizing the rights of others
- Gaining a sense of independence
- Accepting responsibility
- Making decisions
- Learning to compromise
- Becoming aware of safety rules
- Developing the ability to plan ahead
- Learning that mother is not the provider of every need

Use waiting time effectively. Here are ways driving mothers use the time while the children are busy at their activity:

- Maida takes a nap in the car.
- I run and do my errands.
- Pam does her correspondence.
- Kay does her manicure and tweezing.
- One nameless mother spends her time cultivating "friends" who might ultimately become drivers in a car pool.

Expectations What are your children's expectations?

- Are they reasonable?
- Can you meet them?
- Do you want to meet them?

What are your expectations?

- Is the child always ready on time?
- Does the child have all necessary equipment?
- Does the child meet your other personal expectations?
- When does the child inform you of previously arranged commitments?
- Does the child give adequate notice if there is a change of plans?
- Does the child attempt to plan activities around your availability?

Step Four: Positive Effects

Pride
Both parents and children feel a sense of pride in sharing the knowledge that a child is capable and responsible enough to transport himself/herself to an activity.
Self-Reliance
Children learn to trust their judgment by using their judgment. They become self-reliant by doing things for themselves. Walking/biking safely to and from an activity contributes to this self-reliance.
Mutual Respect
Even when a compromise translates to a parent being unable to transport the child to an activity, children learn that they can't have everything. It's a difficult lesson to learn, but when the children gain that insight young, they usually develop respect for other people's needs. Children who get every single thing

they want, even rides, tend to grow up believing that they can have every single thing they want. These children have a greater difficulty in making decisions and compromises and in simply learning that they cannot have everything.

Independence

Both children and parents feel good when children handle appropriate independence.

Step Five: Where I Stand

I believe that

- walking/biking
- car pooling
- bartering for services
- hiring a driver
- using taxis or Dial-a-Ride
- eliminating need

is the best transportation decision I can make at this time because it

- gives me approval
- makes my children happy
- is the cheapest
- leaves me with the most free time
- is the most equitable
- other

Step Six: Act

My immediate plan is to ______________________________.

These are the things I must do to implement my plan.

1. ______________________________
2. ______________________________
3. ______________________________
4. ______________________________
5. ______________________________
6. ______________________________
7. ______________________________

Suggestions.

- Barter one of your talents as a trade-off for driving services.
- Risk rejection but ask for one trip per week from spouse/friends/child, etc.
- Practice the route with your child so that you feel comfortable about safety.
- Rearrange schedules as efficiently as possible.
- Keep telephone numbers of all people involved handy at home and at work.

> Whatever means of transportation you decide is best depends on your own needs. Make it your business, however, to drive with or travel with the person providing the transportation. Check the validity of his or her license and reputation as carefully as you would anyone providing child care. Remember, your child's life and safety are at stake.

Step Seven: Reevaluation

I will reevaluate my transportation decision in ________ weeks/months/semester/duration of job span.

If noticeable changes take place or when something stops working I will:

STOP

ASK WHY?

1. Why isn't it working?
2. What's going wrong?
3. Where's the clog in the wheel?

MAKE CHANGES

1. What change might make things easier?
2. Are all of these complications necessary?
3. Discuss the needed changes with the other people involved in order to come to terms.

TRY ANOTHER ALTERNATIVE

1. There are no simple solutions, only intelligent choices. Start again!

GUILT/ANGER SELF-EVALUATION WORKBOOK

WHERE DOES GUILT COME FROM? It's a fact of life. To some degree or another working mothers feel guilt, and this guilt gets in the way of feeling good about ourselves.

Let's try to identify the source of guilt so we can deal with it effectively. Let's try to:

- Research the source of our guilt.
- Identify the specific situation that makes you feel guilty.
- Modify behavior with the ultimate goal of eliminating guilty feelings.

To reach this goal, each of us must delve into our own personal history. The following workbook pages are designed to help each person better understand her own value. Work through this self-evaluation section and see if it helps identify and, ultimately, eliminate your guilt.

EARLY CHILDHOOD PERSONAL HISTORY

Each family offers its children some degree of love, security, and direction. Children take this, like a package, with them in life when relating to other people. And from this package, each child creates a self-image.

ANSWER THESE QUESTIONS TO DETERMINE HOW YOU FEEL ABOUT YOURSELF

What is your position in the family?
firstborn ______ middle ______ only ______
baby ______ twins ______

Were you the favorite?
your mother's? ______ your father's? ______

As a child, what did you do to please

your mother?	your father?
____________________	____________________
____________________	____________________
____________________	____________________

Today, what do you do to please

your mother?	your father?
____________	____________
____________	____________
____________	____________

Did the same behavior please both parents?

Yes ____________ No ____________

What behavior pleased

your mother?	your father?
____________	____________
____________	____________
____________	____________

Did pleasing one mean displeasing the other?

What you did	Mother pleased	Father pleased
____________	____________	____________
____________	____________	____________
____________	____________	____________
	Mother displeased	Father displeased
____________	____________	____________
____________	____________	____________
____________	____________	____________

Aside from observable signs of affection, what are the ways in which love was shown?

from mother?	from father?
____________	____________
____________	____________
____________	____________

What did you do to secure your position of importance in the family?

as a child	today, with your own family
____________	____________
____________	____________
____________	____________

What did you do when you were criticized or punished?

What you did	What they said
______________________	______________________
______________________	______________________
______________________	______________________

What areas make/made you feel most secure about yourself?

As a child	Suggested responses	Today
______________	school/work	______________
______________	achievement	______________
______________	at home	______________
______________	popularity	______________
______________	hobbies	______________
______________	athletics	______________
______________	social peers	______________
______________	looks	______________
______________	with family	______________

What "unmet needs" do you have left over from your childhood?

____

____

____

In the light of these early childhood experiences, what similarities (if any) do you see in your behavior of today and then?

Today	Then
______________________	______________________
______________________	______________________
______________________	______________________

In looking at your behavior of today, do you find any patterns that you recognize *not* to be in your best interest?

Behavior patterns	Your feelings about them
______________________	______________________
______________________	______________________
______________________	______________________

Do you recognize a behavior that stems from some unmet need of childhood? If so, describe it.

Unmet need	Behavior
______________________	______________________
______________________	______________________
______________________	______________________

Guilt

If you find, from analyzing your own personal history, that you have positive feelings about yourself, the rest of this workbook section may not apply to you. If there are any patterns in your behavior that do not contribute to your positive self-image, however, you may find it of value to answer the following questions.

These observable signs of guilt/anger may serve as obstacles in your path of trying to manage the dual career of homemaker and career woman effectively:

Do you find these symptoms get in your way in being effective at home, at work, or in relating to others?

irritability ______________________

depression ______________________

susceptibility to binges (eating, shopping, drinking to excess)

____

workaholism ______________________

Do you recognize any of these symptoms as an obstacle in combining career and household management?

____

____

____

What do you do to compensate for guilt?
Take tranquilizers ______________________
Eat ______________________
Drink ______________________
Shop ______________________
Work at a hobby ______________________
Keep compulsively busy ______________________

ROLE MODELS AND EXPECTATIONS

This section asks questions to help you explore the role models you have had and the expectations your parents had of you. If you feel guilty or angry it is possible that you feel you are not meeting the expectations of other people. Ideally, the person who finds self-approval rather than approval from others has a better self-image and less guilt. Few working mothers, however, are guilt-free. This section helps you understand how you behave and how you came to believe that this behavior would work in your best interest.

Why do you think these things were/are done?

Why your mother did the things she did	Suggested responses	Why you do what you do for your children
____________	to show love	____________
____________	to be in control	____________
____________	to be needed	____________
____________	it was expected	____________
____________	enjoyment	____________

________	because of anger (or guilt)	________
________	to keep the peace	________

What your mother did for your father	What you do for your mate
________	________
________	________
________	________

Why did your mother do it?	Suggested responses	Why do you do it?
________	financial security	________
________	expectation	________
________	devotion	________
________	self-fulfillment	________

The Good Mother

Perhaps you feel guilt as a working mother because you are not living up to some idealized image you received as a child. Using your own mother as an example, try to determine whether you were presented with a positive or a negative role model of a "good mother."

What did your mother do for you?	Suggested responses	What do you do for your children?
________	shop	________
________	cook	________
________	serve	________
________	clean	________
________	take care of personal needs	________
________	do homework	________
________	do laundry	________

What did your mother do for you?	Suggested responses	What do you do for your children?
______	make and break appointments	______
______	share hobbies	______
______	provide financial support	______
______	act supportive	______
______	provide freedom	______
______	give independence	______
______	instill sense of self-worth	______

EXPECTATIONS

What expectations were set for you in childhood?

From mother	From father
______	______
______	______
______	______

What were your own expectations?

______

______

______

What expectations have you met?

______	of mother?	______
______	of father?	______
______	of self?	______
______	of mate?	______
______	of children?	______

What obstacles have gotten in the way of meeting your expectations? (Put a star next to those you expect to change in the next five years.)

______

______

______

______

APPROVAL

What did/do you do to gain approval from others?*

Then	Suggested responses	Now
________________	tap dance	________________
________________	look pretty	________________
________________	smile	________________
________________	get high grades	________________
________________	volunteer	________________
________________	go to Sunday school and church	________________
________________	wear dresses	________________

What did/do you do to gain approval from yourself?

Then	Now
________________________	________________________
________________________	________________________
________________________	________________________
________________________	________________________

If you found, after answering the above questions, that you are still doing things you did as a child to gain approval, but you don't feel good about doing them (or they make you feel guilty), then it is time to learn to change your behavior. But first, let us continue this self-analysis.

In the light of your early childhood experiences, do you see yourself today, as an adult, behaving in any similar ways to gain approval from others?

____

____

____

*Sexist examples were specifically chosen because this was a life experience shared by most little girls aiming to please.

Do you find any patterns in your behavior today that are not in your best interest (that do not make you feel the best about yourself)?

Do you notice any of those patterns in your personal history?

Can you recognize that you do these things for the same reasons that in your early life led you to get love, approval, security?

WHO YOU ARE

What kind of woman were you expected to be?

As a mother	As a mate

Are you that kind of woman?

As a mother	As a mate

What do you do today to please family members?

Behavior that gives you self-approval	Behavior that contributes to uncomfortable feelings

UNMET NEEDS

Let's try to find out what your mother didn't do for you that now dominates what you choose to do for your children.

What your mother didn't do (unmet needs)	What you do to compensate

How do your children respond to this specific behavior of yours?

What you do to compensate for your unmet needs	What your children say to you when you do it

STRESS

Describe the stress involved when you tried/try to meet other people's expectations

As a child	Now

What do you give your children that your parents did not give you?

________	freedom	________
________	sense of self-worth	________
________	independence	________
________	security	________

What do you *not* give to your children that makes you feel guilt?

________	time	________
________	energy	________
________	security	________
________	stability	________

Under what circumstances do you feel
Anger ________
Stress ________
Anxiety ________
Ill at Ease ________
Fatigue ________

How often do you feel . . . (number of times each day, week, month, year)
anger ________
stress ________
fatigue ________
anxiety ________
phobias ________
uncomfortable ________
guilt ________
frustration ________
depression ________

Which of these physical stress symptoms (which may have an underlying relationship to guilt/anger) do you have?
fatigue ________ insomnia ________
headaches ________ migraine ________

nailbiting ______	obesity ______
chronic eating ______	ulcers ______
back pain ______	hypertension ______
stomachaches ______	colitis ______
chain-smoking ______	alcoholism ______
yelling ______	severe phobias ______

Most of us carry our unmet childhood needs into adulthood. Here's the true story of how one woman brought her own unmet need into adulthood and how it affected her and her family. I call it . . .

The Three O'clock Blues

Recently, I attended a party to celebrate my friend's career advancement. It was a joyous occasion, and everyone shared her success with genuine affection. But it seemed to create a strain for our mutual friend Marcia, who openly complained about her job dissatisfaction. Marcia was the one who always insisted that a mother's duty was to be there after school every day. In fact, over the years, she had made a number of negative innuendoes about career-oriented mothers who weren't at home with their children. I was a bit surprised by her candor that evening! Perhaps it was the wine, or just plain disillusionment. Nevertheless, Marcia's pain directly correlates with the purpose of this section and serves as an introduction to the self-evaluation workbook that follows.

Marcia is a typical worker who spends a great deal of time and energy on the job without ever advancing. The expression "spinning wheels" describes her feeling precisely. Marcia made a decision never to work at a job that didn't allow her to be there for her children by three in the afternoon. She once said that full-time working mothers were detrimental to their children's well-being, and she often announced: "I don't have guilt because I'm home at three o'clock, even if my children aren't."

On this evening, she spoke differently, making it perfectly obvious that she questioned her earlier decisions. She complained that she worked as hard as anyone else in her office but because of her part-time status didn't share in either the salary level or the fringe benefits the others enjoyed. Prompted, I suppose, by a little jealousy of our friend's new position, she said: "Wow, if I had chosen to work full time I'd be earning her salary today." I promptly agreed. We all recognized and supported Marcia's talents and capabilities. But Marcia always resisted the idea of career success by explaining:

"When I was a little girl, even though I was the adored baby of the family, no one was really home for me after school. Even on those days that Mom was home, she wasn't available. So I vowed, no matter what, to be there for my children."

On this evening, at the party, I asked Marcia what was making her so upset. Her honesty jolted me.

"When I started this job, being home by three was my priority. Inside, I knew I would feel guilty if I wasn't there for my kids. The funny thing is that my kids were rarely home. They chose to be involved in scouts or band or art clubs. But I rushed home! I even gave a name to how I felt: I call it the Three O'Clock Blues. It was the same empty feeling I had as a little girl. It makes me so angry with them. I gave up a good career, and they don't seem to appreciate it or me!"

That was it in a nutshell. Marcia's problem illustrates the point of the guilt/anger pattern on which the following workbook pages focus. Let me clarify Marcia's problem for you:

- Marcia has an unresolved childhood conflict with her mother: an unmet need.
- Marcia never recognized that she had this conflict, therefore her anger is suppressed. Yet this one unmet need has dominated her style of mothering for years.
- Marcia has such strong feelings about being there at three o'clock that to avoid her guilt she arranges her life around this priority. Guilt is a double-edged sword! Like Marcia, people sometimes feel guilt because of anger they have suppressed. (Marcia never has said an unkind word about her mother.)

- Her frustrations with her job and with her feelings of not being appreciated by her children provoke additional anger. Now, Marcia openly directs her anger at her children because she rushes home for them and they aren't there. Thus Marcia makes her children feel guilty about participating in activities when they should be enjoying some space to grow. Moreover, when Marcia is upset with her job status, she let it be known that because of the children she sacrificed golden career opportunities.

Thus, the guilt/anger pattern continues. The moral is: Identify whether the need that you are trying to fulfill is your own unmet need (carried over from your childhood) or the actual need of your children today. (Ask them—they'll tell you.)

Perhaps you recognize now that there is something that you've been doing for a long time that is not in your best interest. The reason you are still doing it is probably because you never examined it before. Now that you understand that what you are doing isn't in your best interest, you are free to change, but first you must forgive yourself and not punish yourself just because one of the many things you do isn't working.

Remember . . .

Self-approval = Strong self-image
independent and content

Approval from others = Weaker self-image
dependent and not content

Read on to discover how to prepare for change and to develop a stronger self-image.

POSITIVE CHANGE

This section pinpoints what makes you feel like an accomplished, happy person and what detracts from that feeling. People who always need to get approval from others seem to follow patterns. Frequently, their need creates behavior to compensate for the guilt they feel inside. Often, adults discover that they behave in the same fashion they did as children. When this behavior gets in the way of successfully combining the dual careers of a working woman at home and at her job, change might be in order. Through this self-evaluation, each person can determine an area of change that might help eliminate guilt.

How Can You Tell if You Are the One Who Needs to Change?

If

- You are totally responsible for the well-being of the members of your family

- You are deferring your needs to meet the needs of others more frequently than not
- You are unable to identify your needs
- You are unable to express your needs
- You lack any private leisure time
- You are home, yet drained, at the end of the day
- You have to check with others to find out what you can do
- You talk about other family members when people ask, "How are you?"
- You suffer from chronic stress symptoms
- Your behavior is dominated by unmet needs from childhood

How to Develop a Strong Self-Image

Think about what works well for you, then ask yourself if you constantly have to please other people in order to feel good about yourself. If your answer is "yes," think about adapting or eliminating that behavior to leave more room for the behavior that works well for you and that gives you self-approval. You develop a strong self-image by accepting who you are, and you can bring that positive sense of self with you to your dealings and relationships with other people.

SELF-EVALUATION

Assess your strengths and weaknesses to evaluate yourself.

Strengths	*Weaknesses*
As mother, spouse, worker, friend	
______________________	______________________
______________________	______________________
______________________	______________________
______________________	______________________
______________________	______________________

What do *you* need to do to feel good about yourself?

____
____
____
____
____

What do you need *others* to do to feel good about yourself?

____
____
____
____
____

On whom are you most dependent?
Self ____________________ Others ____________________

Identify your personal attributes (qualities that describe the uniqueness of you).

How others see you	How you see yourself
____________________	____________________
____________________	____________________
____________________	____________________
____________________	____________________
____________________	____________________

If the lists contain more similarities than differences, go on to the next question. If not, try to describe the reason for the differences.

____
____

Which of the qualities you mentioned contributes to unsatisfactory feelings about yourself?

____
____

What would you change if you felt you could?

____

____

List the risks involved in this change:

____

____

____

If you have decided that previously developed patterns are not working for you, and you have determined the risks involved in change, please consider that it may be a greater risk *not* to change. If change is what you're after, please keep in mind that your integrity is more important than the approval of others.

Spend some time looking over what you have written to help you analyze your patterns of behavior. If you recognize yourself as a chronic sufferer of certain stress symptoms and if you now recognize behavior detrimental to your well-being, then you should accept that there is a correlation between your childhood experience and your current adult behavior. Change is in order. Read on to consider how best to effect it.

IDEAS THAT WORK FOR MOTHERS WHO WORK

SOME changes are dramatic, others even traumatic. But most of us make changes in tiny baby steps taken one at a time.

I can remember some of the changes I made that may seem inconsequential to others but that improved my life. Some of them are tiny—like when I gave up making big Sunday breakfasts for the family. It was a need I had because I loved the Sunday bacon and egg breakfasts my father cooked. But Bob would rather work around the house or sail than eat, and the kids preferred to sleep. Finally, they convinced me that I was the only one who cared about Sunday breakfast and I was driving them crazy complaining that they wouldn't come to eat! So—goodbye breakfasts, hello Sunday *Times!*

I hope the ideas in the next section will provoke some little changes in your daily life that will give you more of that one precious commodity that working mothers never have enough of: time.

If these ideas give you some spare time, I'll feel successful. By the way, many of them are my own, and others have been picked up along the way from acquaintances. I keep trying new ones because each year brings different stages and new problems, which require new solutions. Like everything else in the book, I offer them to you as a present; keep them, give them away, or throw them out—it is up to you. I feel they are worthwhile, particularly if you have decided you do too much for everyone and want to figure out how to do less.

Here's a look at some ideas from my "clip and save" file. If you are searching for changes, try some of them!

IDEAS FOR USE OF TIME

Essentially, spending time is like spending money: the more you save the more you have. When you save one hour—by not going grocery shopping this week, for instance—you gain one hour to spend on yourself. If you can do that two or three times a week you will be able to afford the time for all kinds of wonderful luxuries.

Try some of these ideas:

Take the hour you save by not entering your child's room and spend it

- Meeting your favorite person for a drink
- Taking a leisurely bath
- Curled up with a good book

Take the half hour you save every night by not doing dishes and use it to

- Exercise
- Talk with your children
- Chat on the phone with people you are too busy to see
- Put your feet up and read the newspaper

Save up a few hours each week and spend them

- Enjoying a hobby
- Giving yourself a facial, manicure, and/or pedicure
- Listening to music
- Making love!

At 5:30 P.M., health clubs are crowded with working mothers who know that the one hour they spend on themselves there helps them to deal with the family better at 6:30. At the same hour, barstools are occupied by loving wives and mothers who need to relax with a Perrier and lime before starting the next part of their work day. It's not easy to find time or to spend it wisely. Perhaps the following pages will help.

Idea #1: Establish Your Priorities

List the ten things you spend most of your time doing, being sure to include

- What you do for yourself
- What you have to do for others
- What you choose to do for others

List these items in numerical order according to your priorities:

1. ______________________________
2. ______________________________
3. ______________________________
4. ______________________________
5. ______________________________
6. ______________________________
7. ______________________________
8. ______________________________
9. ______________________________
10. ______________________________

Now, ask yourself: Am I spending time and energy doing things for others that (a) I dislike or (b) they don't need/want me to do? If your answer is "yes," move on to Idea #2.

Idea #2: Eliminate

Try to get rid of doing some of the things you hate or some of the things *they* could live without. Ask yourself if any given activity is worth the time and energy you spend doing it.

- Consider some of the meals you prepare. Could you eliminate making Saturday lunch or Sunday breakfast? Could another family member be in charge of a meal or two?
- Organize your household more logically to eliminate work.
- Exchange top sheets, blankets, and spreads for a comforter.
- Use paper plates and cups occasionally.
- Organize storage to eliminate frequent shopping.
- Learn to say, "No, I'm sorry," to people.
- Eliminate people, pets, and meetings that are more aggravating than productive of good feelings.
- Use washable terrycloth towels as curtains in a child's room, kitchen, and bath. They can clip on to the rods and are pretty and maintenance-free.
- Use the dry-cleaner for silk and wool, as I do, or be smarter and buy only wash and wear!
- Make a note of things you do that waste time. Then try to eliminate that behavior. (I could spend an hour a week lazing around if I added the minutes I waste searching for my keys!)

Idea #3: Organize Time Efficiently

Teachers, like working mothers, need to organize time efficiently. In one forty-two-minute class period, I do many of the following: take attendance, check homework, try to introduce new work, have students read or speak aloud in the foreign language, show slides or a movie, give or correct a test, and give a homework assignment.

If you consider how many activities you complete in one busy working hour you will find that you are capable of using time efficiently. When you make your daily/weekly/monthly "to do" lists, consider these ideas to help organize your time more efficiently.

Consider your own body. Plan tasks according to your own biological clock. Do the most difficult tasks when you have the most energy.

Consider options and limitations. Do you have a baby who naps? Are others busy when you are free? Plan your schedule accordingly to fit your tasks into those time slots.

Plan your time and budget it as carefully as thrifty people budget money. If you must attend a function, can you arrive late and leave early and still fit in your priority activity?

Consolidate activities. Route errands as efficiently as you would if scheduling deliveries was your job. Make all telephone calls at one time. Prepare many meals at once.

Learn to say, "I'm busy right now," to avoid unneccessary interruptions.

Set a deadline. give yourself a date by which time a task must be completed.

Use labor-saving devices. You already know about using other people; now make a list of objects that will help you save time. Try to purchase them.

Double up on activities. Sort mail while on the telephone, write the list or letter while waiting in the car, clean a purse while waiting in line, exercise while watching TV, study a foreign language from a cassette tape while driving.

Idea #4: Illustrate Your Use of Time

I'm not sure how or why I discovered the following idea, but it really made a difference for me. My priorities became crystal clear the first time I did this.

1. Make a large circle.
2. Divide the circle into wedges representing the proportions of time you spend. (It should look like the "pie" illustrations of government tax dollars.)
3. Superimpose a second pie that illustrates the way you would like to be spending your time.
4. Your conclusions should become vivid.
5. Make changes.

Do phone calls interrupt you?

Do you get caught up watching TV for hours?

Do you find days drifting by when you don't accomplish anything?

Do you leave work late each night?

Another way to illustrate your use of time is to create an honest daily plan for yourself. These three steps will make obvious just how often those days, hours, and minutes drift away.

1. Write down the way you spend time.
2. Take a close, hard look at those wasted hours.
3. Keep a diary for a week and a month. (Dieters and people starting budgets find this useful.)

In college, I was taught to make a study plan to maximize the use of time during the week before exams. The dean made a seven-day chart and divided each day into class hours, study hours, free time, and eating and sleeping time. I discovered for the first time just how many periods of time could be scheduled in a day. I think it was the most important lesson I learned at the College of William and Mary!

7–8 A.M.	personal
8–9 A.M.	breakfast
9–11:30 A.M.	classes
11:30 A.M.–1 P.M.	study in library
1–2 P.M.	lunch
2–4 P.M.	class
4–5 P.M.	free
5–6:30P.M.	study in library
6:30–8 P.M.	dinner
8–10 P.M.	study in library
10–12 P.M.	study or hang out
12 P.M.–7 A.M.	sleep

Planning days in time periods works! Here's what I do in an effort to use time even more effectively:

Each month I make a "to do" list for each of my activities: work, family, writing, social, and so on. My yearly calendar typically looks like this:

- January to April: Work, exercise, write, make Passover
- May: Work, sail weekends, family birthdays and anniversaries
- June: Busiest at school! Clear calendar of everything else
- July to August: July Fourth Fireworks Party! Write Monday to Thursday; sail Friday to Sunday
- September: Busy with school!
- October: Leave evenings free for campaigns until election day
- November: Work, write, do Thanksgiving
- December: Work, holidays week, family and social time

I don't attempt to write during the two busy school months but make it a full-time activity on school vacations. I clearly separate work time, family time, writing, and social or special event time.

I divide each week into activity periods:

- Monday to Friday: Work, children, errands, house, meetings, writing

- Saturday and Sunday: Family, social, writing

I give each activity specific days and blocks of time:

- Family: when needed and dinner through evening
- Household chores: Monday and Thursday 3–6 P.M..
- Errands: Tuesday and Friday 5–6 P.M..
- Exercise: Tuesday and Friday 3:30–5 P.M..
- Writing: Saturday and Sunday 10–4 P.M. (School year)

Monday to Thursday 9–3 P.M. (summer)

I still divide each day into blocks of time as I was taught in college:

- Prework 6–7:30 A.M.
- Work 8 A.M.–3 P.M.
- After work 3–7 P.M. I appreciate the good fortune of having this huge block of time in the middle of the day. These used to be "mothering" hours; now I spend them writing.
- Dinner 7–8 P.M.
- Evening 8–11 P.M.

When you divide your day into blocks of time and create schedules for yourself, even though they change according to your family and workloads, you'll find that you'll be more likely to schedule those precious hours for what you want to do.

Try it! Divide your day into five blocks of time, subdividing those if necessary:

- Prework time:
- Work time:
- Household time:
- Children time:
- Meal time:

Create a daily plan like the one you made for your sitter:

7–9 A.M. ______________	1–3 PM. ______________
9–12 A.M. ______________	3–5 P.M. ______________
12–1 P.M. ______________	5–7 P.M. ______________
	8–11 P.M. ______________

Idea #5: Delegate

If you are not aware that learning to delegate will help you manage your life more successfully at home, perhaps this information will convince you. The reason, it is often said, that women don't climb as high up the executive ladder as men is because women don't delegate responsibility as effectively as men do. Those of us who are aware of the reasons why women work so hard to be "good" girls, "good" wives, "good" mothers, and "good" workers often do not realize that such behavior actually hinders success at work as well as at home. If you are now ready to start learning to delegate effectively, I have some ideas to offer you.

- Reread about Pam (the Administrator); her skillful ideas should be tried.
- Make your expectations known in writing (see household rosters pp. 106–109) after discussing them
- Negotiate from strength. After all, you pay the household helpers and you give to your children. Your reasonable and considerate expectations should be met.
- If you want to keep your marriage working *while* you are working, I would not delegate to your husband. Equal partners share. You delegate to those who work for you or whom you teach (like children).
- To delegate means to direct effectively with open communication. It does not mean slave-driving; it does not mean commanding others to do tasks, no questions asked. It is an effective way to direct other people to do agreed-upon chores.
- Understand that what you delegate, and to whom you delegate, will change periodically.
- If you equate delegating with ordering people around, and you find that difficult, make lists of suggestions and keep them posted.
- Once you delegate a task, let it go.

- Concentrate not on *how* it is done, but *that* it is done.
- Praise the completed task rather than criticize the imperfections.

Idea #6: Use Phone Time Effectively

Ma Bell's Umbilical Cord

The telephone cord links us to our children like a substitute umbilical cord, providing emotional nourishment. From office desk, restaurant pay phones, and even from bedside, we ring: "Hello darling, is everything OK?"

What working mother has not felt the pang of fear when the unexpected call disturbs her at work? Who among us has not sighed with relief when the crisis was minor? Who has not felt the pride when one of our children makes an independent, intelligent decision on the spur of the moment?

These scenarios are shared by millions of working mothers. And those phone calls, whether we realize it or not, epitomize one of the most useful tools for the working mother: to give emotional support and to share activities by phone, to enhance the children's sense of security and their independence at the same time, is to make the most of your dual career life.

MOTHERING BY PHONE

- Do your children know where to reach you?
- If they cannot call you, do you call them at a scheduled time?
- Are you supportive via the phone?
- Does your voice convey your feelings?
- Do you ask relevant questions that elicit more than a "yes" or "no" response?

HELPFUL HINTS

- Keep lists of important telephone numbers available for your children, as well as for your mother-substitutes.
- Insert time availability on lists:
  "call between 3 and 3:15"
  "call on the hour"
- Plan a scheduled time each day (when your teenagers spare ten minutes from settling the love-life problems of the world) when the lines are free for you.
- Teach your children that brevity is necessary; they cannot leave the phone to pet the cat on your business time.
- Display discipline, assurance, caring, and concern—say it with love.

PROFESSIONALIZE YOUR HOME PHONE

- Teach *everyone who writes* how to write the names and numbers of callers. Teach everyone who speaks how to answer the phone. If the person cannot take a message, teach these three words: Please call again!
- Always have a message pad and pencil (nailed, if you must) available.
- Screen calls: "May I ask what this is in reference to?"
- Memorize this statement: "I'm sorry, I'm busy right now. When can I call you back?"
- Like the pediatrician, let your associates, family, and friends know what times they should call.
- Make a song out of it if you must, but teach all children, even toddlers, to say:
  HELLO. THIS IS ______.
  (S)HE CANNOT COME TO THE PHONE NOW.
  PLEASE CALL BACK. (toddlers)
  PLEASE LEAVE NAME AND NUMBER. (Older children)
  THANK YOU. GOOD-BYE.
  Practice with a play and real phone and praise galore! It is excellent skill-building for older children to write numbers and remember to keep messages.

TELEPHONE MEMO

Mom at work	_____	_______
Dad at work	_____	_______
Grandparents	_____	_______
Neighbor	_____	_______
Friend	_____	_______
Doctor	_____	_______
Police	_____	_______
Poison	_____	_______
School	_____	_______

Phone free 4:00–4:15 p.m.
Message taker says:
"Hello, this is _____.
(S)he cannot come to the phone now.
Please leave your name and number.
Thank you. good-bye."

Idea #7: Make Time for You

When you get a headache, or when you feel sorry for yourself and droopy all over, it's time to listen to your body and make time for you. Do what you'd do for your children or even for your plants if they were drooping. Pretty soon you'll be sparkling again.

Try at least one of these gifts to yourself:

- Call in sick and take a mental health day off from work, or take a day off from the household. Stay in bed, say you have a viral infection (it sounds more serious than a cold), take the phone off the hook and put a"DO NOT DISTURB" sign on the bedroom door.
- Keep the sitter and call the beauty salon. Spend the morning getting or giving yourself a manicure, pedicure, and/or facial.
- Go to a movie *alone*.
- Get thee to a library and indulge. Read the book you've been itching to start.
- Call your mother/sister/friend and, instead of saying, "Hi," say "Help!"
- Make a reservation for dinner at your favorite restaurant.
- Make a reservation at a sexy hotel and surprise your mate.
- Join a health club or exercise class and work on your body or start a diet.

Whatever you do, remind yourself that you deserve the indulgence!

IDEAS FOR SHOPPING

My food-shopping hints are biased by a total distaste for the supermarket: the lines, the carts (don't you agree that aisles should be one way to avoid collisions?), the packages, ad infinitum. The day I realized that it was a total waste of energy to spend an hour or more a week buying two cans of tuna and three bars of soap, I started plotting. These hints are based upon years of avoidance techniques. Even as I type, I am avoiding the supermarket. It is snowing, a wet, slushy snow. My refrigerator has no milk, no eggs, and only enough orange juice for a baby. So, you ask, why are you typing? Because, I hate to shop.

I called the butcher, who carries meat, eggs, and cookies, and, since it was too late for a delivery, my husband agreed to pick up the order. I think it's fair. He refuses to find milk when it *is* in the refrigerator, and these days I cook, serve, and even (now, when the children are out more than in) clean up from dinner. We each serve coffee to the other in bed. Today, I brought him juice and breakfast in bed. So when I suggested that I was busy, and he suggested that he needed food, he went to the butcher. In a perfect partnership perhaps I wouldn't have to say anything at all. But ours is only 99$^{44}/_{100}$ths perfect.

Idea #1: Give the Shopping Chores to Someone Else

Oh, yes, you can! If you are willing to relinquish some control, it is fairly easy to have other people shop. Kids often love to shop for their own clothing, food, and school supplies. Sure, they might not do as well as you at first, but experience is the best educator. If you help them make up their lists you are not only doing yourself a favor but training them to be responsible and independent.

Husbands, who often resent doing cleaning chores, seem to find shopping an acceptable task. If your spouse fits into that category, let him be responsible for provisioning. Some women really underestimate men in this capacity and talk about bright men as if they were idiots. If they need lists and instructions, so did you at first. If they make mistakes, laugh it off as the price of experience. Otherwise, the first shopping expedition will be the last. Your attitude determines whether someone else will do the work.

Household workers, particularly those who are proud of their shopping skills, often shop for me. Sitters and drivers used to shop. I came out even: their coupon savings equaled the extra salary cost. Besides, they buy only what is on a list. I save a lot of dollars that way! I always encourage cleaning help to buy all of the cleaning supplies. They usually brag about their bargains and get the brands *they* like to use.

Trade off use of the car or a new sweater for shopping chores. I call it motivation, others call it bribery. Whatever it's called, it's very effective.

Dr. Joyce Brothers suggests that by the age of five, children should be learning to make their own clothing decisions. She claims that it teaches independent decision making, and I most certainly concur. By the time children reach the preteen stage, they should be making most, if not all, of their personal purchases themselves. Not only will they learn the value of money and how to spend it, but they will enjoy their possessions more.

They might even take better care of them. You gain the benefit of relinquishing another responsibility to the person to whom it rightfully belongs.

Idea #2: Shop in Bulk

About once a month, or whenever the cupboards are bare, or I've just been paid, or there is a double coupon special, I put on sneakers and go to the supermarket. Shop like a restaurant manager: fill up the basket with basic supplies. I buy only the most economical sizes, as much as I can pay for and store. Once, before our annual Fourth of July party, I spent a good portion of my summer paycheck at the supermarket, the paper goods discount place, the soda and beer warehouse, and the liquor store. It seemed expensive at the time, but in retrospect, I saved plenty. I had coffee on the shelf at $1.99 a can long after the stores were charging $3. Moreover, a radio program once suggested that the best investment middle-income people could make was to beat inflation by buying in bulk. Then, they said, you actually save the difference between what you spent and what it would have cost. Be that as it may, it works for me. Even when I had minimal funds, I shopped monthly. I avoided impulse buying and saved time as well as money.

Clip coupons, wait for the double coupon specials, then *shop*. Avoid buying gimmicks—put those coupons in the garbage. But if you want to save money with coupons, do a coupon shopping trip systematically:

- Use a coupon organizer for easy access
- Don't shop for everything else, only coupon items
- Use a list detailing the coupons' requirements.

Idea #3: Shop on Vacation

At any given time, I can tell where I've been by what I'm wearing. I have lots of time to shop on vacations and can find good buys. By coordinating all the separates I own (I buy black and beige), it is fairly easy to build up a wardrobe by adding a new touch to the oldies but goodies I've found somewhere.

People who are *really* clever buy holiday gifts on vacation. I do that, too, but I usually give them, use them, or lose them before holiday time. But don't do as I do, do as I suggest!

One of my friends uses one of her vacation days to shop for food. It may not sound like fun to you, but she equips her household with supplies that last her the season. Consider your own schedule. Perhaps one four-hour period spent when you are relaxed, not rushed, is worth not having to shop for household supplies for the next six months. If you can spare a vacation day or if you can't get away and you can pay, it's worth a try.

Besides, if you shop in the morning, you can still reserve "vacation time" for the afternoon. Go to the beauty salon and splurge. Get a facial, manicure, pedicure, and new hairdo. Or go clothes shopping for yourself. Then meet your favorite person for dinner and consider yourself "on vacation."

Idea #4: Shop on Sale, by Mail!

- My husband, an inveterate catalog reader, does all of his equipment shopping in the lavatory. He is a walking information source of catalog prices. He waits, comparison shops, and buys on sale, by mail.

- Dorothy, who did everything so well, shopped for her baby's needs on sale, by mail. Although some high-priced stores have catalogs, nobody suggests that those are the only ones. Department store circulars announce bargains, as do many newspapers. But don't ever buy something you should try on first unless you do business with a reputable mail order firm that has 800 numbers and easy return policies. Gifts, accessories, and household replacements are easily ordered with a postcard or a toll-free telephone call.
- Select standard gifts for different occasions: wine glasses for weddings, tool boxes for high school graduates, books for hostesses, jewelry for daughters' or friends' birthdays. Call toll-free, charge it, and have the gift delivered.
- When I was twelve, I ran away from home for a few hours and spent them in my friend's attic. I had sixty-three comic books, one jar of peanut butter, a jar of jelly (even then I brought food with me), and milk and bread. What impressed me during that lonely afternoon (when I punished my mother by running away and sat miserably alone) was that the attic was filled with cartons of toilet paper, paper towels, soap, shampoo, and other supplies. They came from a big city department store. My friend, whose mother worked full time (that's why I ran away to her house) was a clever shopper. She knew in 1950 how to shop on sale, by mail.

Idea #5: Shop Seasonally

Try to buy (on sale) after the season; buy in bulk.

- In January, when everyone is all "spent out," necessities go on sale.
- Buy socks and underwear by the dozen. Get the same identifiable socks for each person. That way, I finally learned,

you can catch the sock thieves. I wear only solid black, blue, or brown. They don't.
- Make a special date and shop for your child once a season. Go for lunch and treat it as a treat, not a chore!
- Buy household supplies on sale in January or August.
- Buy next year's holiday items at the sales immediately after the holiday.

P.S. If you buy stripes or argyles, for heaven's sake buy many alike. The washing machine monster eats socks, and it is a pain to have two perfect socks in different colors or patterns. (Perhaps your family will wear an unmatched set and start a new fad, but mine won't.) Also, have you ever noticed that out of fifteen white socks, no two have the same colored stripes?

Idea #6: Use a List Stating Brand Names and Sizes

If you delegate shopping to other people (and this is the easiest chore to delegate), a detailed list makes life simpler. First, it reduces the chance of error. Second, your shopper might choose brands you detest. Avoid mistakes that cause conflicts by giving clear instructions.

I learned from my children when I yelled at them for buying the wrong thing. They told me in no uncertain terms that they were trying to help and that my attitude made them feel angry and unappreciated. Parents who question, scold, or otherwise imply that the shopper didn't do a good job will lose a shopper. You can avoid conflict by making clear copies of your list. Always keep a copy posted so that family members jot down what items are missing or needed.

AISLE BY AISLE SHOPPING LIST

LEFT WALL
vegetables ________
____
____
____
fruits ________
____
____
____

AISLE 1
cleaning supplies ________
____
____
____
____

AISLE 2
pet supplies ________
____
____

AISLE 3
party snacks ________
____
soda ________
____
cards ________
____

AISLE 4
baby supplies ________
____

AISLE 5
health/beauty ________
____
____
____

BACK
meat ________
fish ________
chicken ________

AISLE 6
paper/plastic ________
____

FRONT
breads ________
____
____
____

AISLE 7
frozen foods ________
____
ice cream ________
____
____

AISLE 8
canned fruits ________
____
canned vegetables ________
____
____
health foods ________
____
____
gourmet ________
____

AISLE 9
pasta ________
____
tomato products ________
____
oil ________
vinegar ________

COUPONS
____
____
____

AISLE 10
juices ________ ________ ________ ________

OTHER ________ ________ ________ ________ ________ ________

AISLE 11
cereal ________ ________ ________

baking supplies ________ ________ ________

crackers ________ ________

cookies ________ ________

AISLE 12
jellies ________ ________

peanut butter ________
mustard ________
condiments ________ ________ ________

RIGHT WALL
deli ________ ________ ________ ________ ________

dairy ________ ________ ________ ________ ________

Make a list aisle by aisle if you shop in one favorite place. I learned this from my former high school guidance counselor, a clever man who convinced my mother to allow me to transfer colleges to be near a boy friend. He said there was more chance of us breaking up if we were near each other than if we were pining away at a distance. He was right—we did! He's right about this grocery list, too. It's the easiest list to use because you don't wander back and forth and up and down because of a haphazard list.

Idea #7: Find Stores that Provide Service (Specialty Stores Don't Have to Be Expensive)

To tell the truth, one of the ways I avoid supermarkets is by trying to buy as many items as possible in discount specialty supply houses where service is graciously given.

The following items can be purchased easily, in bulk, from stores that offer the services I enjoy: (a) they deliver; (b) they carry out:

Beer and soda distributors. I can always send someone to buy those items.

Pet supplies. Even if I drive there, an employee or my children carry out.

Household supplies. I try to buy from a distributor who delivers the largest sizes of fine goods.

Automotive. If I must, I go to the shop; they find it and carry out.

Health and beauty aids. I like to do my own shopping for these, although each member of my family either purchases his or her own or gives me a list of wants. I buy at discount beauty supply shops or at my beauty salon, where I pay through the nose.

Produce, meat, fish. I buy produce at the farmer's market or farm stand, fish at the dock or fish store, and meat from the butcher. If I were rich, I think I would buy at the luxury places and get all the wonderful cheeses, breads, and goodies available only in large cities like New York and affluent communities. But I make do locally, and I love chatting with the owners of these places. It has paid off handsomely. They deliver to me, they have been known to pick out my produce, or, if I shop during my break from work, store my goods in their refrigerator while I work. I have been known to meet friends and go for a drink after shopping and storing the groceries. Then I pick it all up (they carry). It pays to be a good customer if you like service.

Nonperishables. Use a restaurant supply house and buy giant-sized mayonnaise, salad dressing, pickles, and spices that don't quickly lose their flavor.

Frozen food/meat plans. I tried one and found it an expensive, though practical, convenience. I suggest that you try one at least for a while and see if it works for you. It was great when I was a busy mother feeding three kids, a mother's helper, and us. But, with a small family, I'd rather patronize my butcher.

IDEAS FOR MEALS

Idea #1: Don't Do It

The idea is very simple, and the choice is yours. You can

1. Do it yourself, spend a great deal of effort, and love or resent it,
2. Pay for someone else to do it, and once you find the right someone, know it will be done well (and that you are free of the chore), or
3. Eliminate the need by not doing it at all.

Since a great deal of this book concerns the price tag of doing it all yourself, and much of the text shows you how and why to delegate chores to others, let's concern ourselves only with the third idea. *Don't do it at all.* When you can, cook triple or more. Buy a Seal-A-Meal for freezing and storing; then boil in water or cook in the microwave. You'll have no pots to clean and time left over, too. And dessert's a breeze if you go out and buy a home-baked or store-bought pie—or no pie at all. Just an hour ago, I received a call from a woman I knew during our first year of marriage. In a short phone call, I learned that her first baby is married and that she had two more children and stayed at home for fifteen years. Since then, she has become very successful. In fact, it was when I noticed her picture in the *New York Times* that I placed the first phone call to her. When she asked what I was doing, I mentioned the book and this section in particular. She laughed. "I haven't cooked a meal in seven years. I haven't been inside a supermarket for seven years!" I, too, laughed. Twenty-three years ago, when we were not yet twenty, this young woman used to bake devotedly for her family. Then she discovered a bakery whose products made her father-in-law flip; he thought she baked them herself. Now she doesn't even bother with that little deception. She, too, went from home-baked, to store bought, to no pie, just as I did.

Idea #2: Save Time and Energy

These ideas are simple and logical to me, but most people don't bother to save time and energy just because it hasn't occurred to them *not* to do something. What could be simpler.

I know that one of my friends has no food in the house (and wastes no time grocery shopping) because she eats out every single night. When, or if, she eats in, she has it delivered. But I love to cook (sometimes) and couldn't possibly live that way. Most working mothers eat out occasionally, but even so, they are responsible for three or four meals a week. Naturally, I'm assuming you have already delegated the making of lunch and breakfast. No? OK. Here are some classic ideas for the very busy person who wants to simplify meals.

Breakfast. Very young children can prepare their own *if* they have individual size servings of cereal and milk. You can either pay for smaller packages or have a sitter play the dividing game. The game goes like this: the sitter and children divide one giant, economy-size box of cereal into many little plastic-covered bowls. Then, when breakfast time comes, a little tyke can remove the bowl from the shelf and pour milk. The sitter, older sibling, or father can use the same game to divide the milk into little plastic bottles.

Snacks. Buy, or have your sitter prepare, little bags of fruit, vegetables, raisins, and the like. Naturally, it costs more to buy, so be sure to ask your sitter, who probably will not mind doing this and perhaps turning the chore into games for counting, sorting, singing, and, of course, eating.

Lunch. Lunch can be healthy with hard-cooked eggs, apples, cheese, tuna from a can, frozen pizzas, and the like. The choice is unlimited. Naturally, it is more convenient for adults and older children to eat at work or in school or to have fun-time foods on weekends. Kids love the fast-food chains, and parents might enjoy them, too. I gave up Saturday and Sunday lunches about ten years ago, and nobody seemed to miss me. The only trouble used to be finding a salad bar for me, but now fast-food restaurants all have them.

School lunch. Each child has his/her own food habits. As a general rule, a child is more likely to eat a lunch he/she has prepared with individual choices. Ask your child about the school lunches. If "Yuck" is the response, you can be sure your hard-earned dollars are being spent on potato chips and chocolate. (Many schools still serve trash because it is profitable.) Lunch belongs to your children, so help them to make intelligent choices about it.

Dinner ideas are unlimited. We all know about restaurants, but if you are lucky enough to eat in them, make it a general rule *never ever* to eat in a restaurant what you can easily prepare at home. Therefore, I buy the best steaks to cook at home. My husband, who swears he can't cook, thinks that barbecues are fun. He'll cook a steak on the outdoor grill anytime, even in deepest winter. He'll also barbecue ribs (which my butcher precooks and marinates), chicken, and other foods.

P.S. I often take a doggy bag home, but the dog doesn't eat the leftovers—I do.

Idea #3: Avoid a Mess
If It Doesn't Get Dirty, No One Has to Clean!

If you have to serve dinner but hate to clean pots, adopt some of these tricks.

- Use a microwave. Vegetables go from plate to table, potatoes get done in five minutes, frozen food goes on paper plates.
- Put your gas grill or barbecue near the kitchen door and use it all year long.
- If you ever get to the point that you can pay for convenience without wincing, find a deli or butcher that sells prepared dishes. Mine makes stuffed pork chops and chicken cordon bleu ready for the oven, precooks and marinates spareribs, and sells pepper steak ready to be cooked. Dinner time is simpler.
- Cook double, triple, and more! Then buy a Seal-A-Meal, save, and store.
- Simplify by using one-dish meals.
- Serve sandwiches on one large tray.
- Use little straw individual baskets (you'll find them at Woolworth's), lined with paper napkins, for finger-lickin' meals like hamburgers, hot dogs, sandwiches, or chicken.

Idea #4: Share Mealtime Responsibilities

It's hard to let go of the idea that you, and only you, are responsible for the shopping, cooking, serving, and cleaning associated with mealtime. Frankly, it's very hard to let go of the one area of the household that many working mothers (including myself) cling to. But I've managed to change, and so can you.

- Meet and discuss the idea of sharing cooking (if you have a cooperative family).
- Delegate one meal per week to each capable person (your husband?).
- Permit catch-as-catch-can meals occasionally.
- Teach another family member to cook.
- If it's another person's turn, and he or she chooses take-out pizza, enjoy it!

You've heard this all before, but if it hasn't worked, try manipulation. Take a class, work late, or meet a friend just so you come home *after* dinnertime. They'll survive, and I'll bet you anything they'll eat, too!

Idea #5: Find a Salad Bar

What I said before about hating supermarkets was true *until* our local supermarkets added a few irresistible services that save time, money, and calories. The following basic meals are as fast and as cheap as those sold at fast-food places. They take minimum preparation and cleanup and are healthy. Each of them makes use of the best value ever: the supermarket salad bar.

- If you like stir-fried veggies but hate to peel, slice, cut, chop, and clean up, stop at the supermarket salad bar and load up on prepared fresh vegetables to throw into your wok or skillet.
- Use the cut-up peppers, mushrooms, onions, and broccoli and cook with whatever meat or fish you prefer. To stretch this meal I either make pasta or buy rice at a take-out Chinese restaurant.
- Shop at the salad bar and add deli meats and cheese for an instant no-work chef's salad.
- Buy barbecued chickens (I call the deli and they are ready when I arrive so I don't have to wait in line) and salad.
- Serve salad and fruit from the salad bar with a microwaved baked potato and charcoal grilled meat. Instant meal!
- Microwave (or steam or sauté) the fresh veggies and add to pasta for a wholesome pasta primavera, or pop them in a pita pocket for an instant meal!

IDEAS FOR CHILDREN

These ideas, and many more, offer mothers an opportunity to give their children the valuable experience of learning to become secure in the knowledge that they can make decisions. This, in turn, gives them self-assurance, self-reliance, and independence. Children who have those qualities often grow up to be the most successful people.

In a world where teachers complain that children would rather sit back and be entertained, where employers complain that young people don't want to work but just to be paid, we, the parents, must consider why. Primarily, it is because young people don't often have to contribute to their families. In earlier generations, children contributed their share from the very youngest years. It is my opinion, supported by research, that young people who learn to be responsible become more capable adults.

Naturally, you, the mother, have to have an attitude of willingness to let go, to offer your child space to do for himself or herself. If you believe that in addition to being a mother you want to be the best mother and the best person for yourself, you will consider adopting some of these ideas.

The time to make changes is *now*. This is the time to sit down, discuss, assess, and reevaluate your behavioral patterns. Help guide and love your children, but be their teacher, not a servant. These ideas work for mothers who work—try them!

Idea #1: Learn to Involve the Kids

Historically, women have not been skilled at delegating. They tend to do everything themselves. This section concentrates on illustrating how you can delegate chores to your children, even to toddlers. If you learn now, you will be light years ahead of the other mothers who fumbled and juggled, nagged and cried to get their children's cooperation. In turn, the children will benefit by becoming independent and pleased with their accomplishments.

Some of the techniques that teachers use to teach effectively are absolutely perfect for you when you start to delegate. They include

- Make learning fun.
- Keep realistic expectations.
- Give clear-cut, well-defined directions.
- Praise lavishly.
- Avoid criticism.

Idea #2: Don't Teach Your Children to "Help Mommy"

When you applaud your children and thank them for helping Mommy, you reinforce the idea that the job *belongs* to Mommy. I don't believe it does. If you want your children to grow up believing that the mess belongs to the person who made it, the dirty clothes belong to the person who dirtied them, and the responsibility belongs to each individual, then don't teach them that they are helping Mommy. Try these ideas instead:

- Praise your children for keeping their rooms so neat.
- Applaud them for making such a good snack for themselves.
- Thank them for picking things up before anyone tripped over them.
- Appreciate them for doing a good job because they are such good workers.
- Help them to feel good about being part of a family effort.

In other words, you can build your child's self-esteem by appreciating what is done for other people and for himself or herself. This way, children can learn to be part of a family team in which each person contributes and appreciates the others.

Idea #3: A Child's Room Belongs to the Child

There are only two ways to assure a neat, clean room in which your children can grow. Of the two, only one works. You can do it all, clean the drawers, hang the clothes, pick everything up off the floor, and put things away. This will work until your child rebels and decides to live in a mess. Then you can either shut the door and ignore the mess, or you can fight. But fighting takes much more energy than it is worth.

I propose that you teach your children from infancy to be responsible for their own clothes, bed, laundry, and especially toys. That way the children find out early that if they wish to live in a neat, clean environment they will have to do the work themselves. And if they seem to prefer a mess, you still win because you are spared the time, energy, and aggravation of doing it all.

Here are some ideas that work:

- When your children go into their first bed, buy a washable sleeping bag and encourage them to straighten the bed. Praise them, don't criticize, or they'll hate to do it.
- Build low shelves and allow the children to arrange their toys in their own way, not yours.
- Get low hooks so helpers can hang their own p.j.'s and jackets.
- Treat blocks like a puzzle, making a game of putting them away.
- Hang stuffed animals on bright ribbons all over the walls on low hooks.
- Let your child trip and fall over a toy, or allow yourself to trip. They can also learn safety lessons through trial and error.

Idea #4: Make Chores into Fun and Games— Kids Will Want to Do Them

Many of the repetitive chores around the house can be shared by little people who adore doing them if you make them fun. Try starting your children out with some of these ideas:

- Teach a toddler to set a table by coloring in shapes on a plain white paper place mat. First, you draw the shape of a fork, knife, spoon, plate, glass, and so on, then give your little one plastic utensils to put in the proper places. Soon your child will want to set the table for everyone.

- Youngsters make wonderful helpers in policing the area inside and out. Use an old pillowcase (please avoid using plastic bags with children), and let your child pick up toys and trash left around the house. Outside, you might have to watch out for glass, but picking up things should be a safe chore in a house or around the yard. Toddlers can learn to feel important this way and learn to like the feeling of work.
- Try the match game with socks! Let a little one try to match the socks and find two alike. This is a wonderful job to give away because parents tend to hate it and children find it a challenge. If your washing machine eats socks, you'll have a little problem. But if they are all together, let a child rummage through. Congratulations are in order when everything gets matched. (Buy a half dozen alike and life is easier!)
- Hang a shoe bag on your child's door. Fill each pocket with picture-coded 5 x 7 cards of chores to do. Your child can help cut out and paste pictures on cards. As an incentive, add bonus cards. For example, a toothbrush means "Brush your teeth." But a picture of a book means you'll read a story after chores. Surprise your child with an occasional picture of a special toy or of a place he or she would like to visit. It's a fun way to make early chores pleasant!

Idea #5: Help Your Youngsters to Dress Independently

One of the nicest things little ones can do for themselves is to choose their clothing and learn to dress. Even toddlers can choose their clothing if you prepare them by planning well.

- Keep solid-colored bottoms in a drawer with printed tops. If you buy color-coordinated items, any top will go with any bottom. Even a little child can enjoy choosing what to wear within these limitations! (This helps enormously when a sitter changes your child's clothes.)
- Buy socks by the half dozen or dozen. Get them all alike. Encourage your children to choose them and to find two.
- Use low hooks on the wall so that as soon as a child can reach the hook he/she can hang a jacket.
- Get two hampers for your children's room and play a game putting white clothes into one and colored objects into the other. Children will love learning about colors this way, and they will be well on their way to doing their own laundry.
- Avoid uncomfortable or difficult clothing. Keep your expectations realistic. If you want to have children who can dress themselves, they certainly can't cope with tight collars or fancy buttons or leotards with seams. Loose tops, snaps, and easy clothes help them not to feel frustrated.
- Encourage youngsters to participate in shopping for their own clothes as preschoolers.

IDEAS FOR SPACE

With the entire family, plus sitters, using the household, the best way to find things is to organize. Household organization is composed of two ideas:

- Everything should have its own place.
- Everything should be put back in its place.

In our household we have become experts at the former, but since only one member (my husband) is consistent about the latter, we still hear this question a lot: "*Where's the* _____ *?*" I'm never quite certain that it is *there,* but I can finally say that I know where it *should* be! Rather than jump to find it, I usually encourage the "looker" to search for it.

Organizing space, like seeking a job or cooking a meal, starts out with two magic ingredients: pencil and paper.

- Make a list of the activities you want each space to serve.
- Then list each necessary item for every activity.
- Separate the most frequently used items and activities from those seldom used and plan storage accordingly.

- List all items that could be considered safety hazards and plan safe storage.
- List valuables and plan accordingly. Your children are your most valuable possessions so plan their room locations and all storage with them in mind.

Organizing takes more skill than money, but some things are important enough to be considered necessities even if they have to be purchased.

Filing cabinet. This is your first major organizational purchase. A box with folders could serve the purpose. After all, where do you put your lists until you create all the storage

Business of life desk. It doesn't matter if you use a shelf in the hall or in a closet, a kitchen work counter, a desk in the living room, or a real office. I've moved my space so often that I once used to sing: "In my own little corner on my own little chair . . ." as a wishful theme song. What matters isn't where it is, but rather that you have a control station from which you can organize this business of life.

A loose-leaf binder to be kept available as a public document for everyone's use. Keep household rosters, shopping lists, lists of people in the kids' clubs, neighbors, repair people, and timetables, bus schedules, people's schedules, and even take-out menus. Add envelope pages to the notebook to store coupons, receipts, and school memos until you file them.

A key rack so that everyone can find keys the minute they are needed.

A message board so everyone will know one place to look for the important messages and notes.

Idea #1: Organize Space to Suit the Children

Kitchen

- Do what grocery stores do: place all necessary items within reach, so children can help themselves and help the household. No law says glasses and dishes should be in the top cabinets.
- Keep napkins, silverware, and condiments within easy reach so children can set the table.
- Post a list on the inside door of the cabinet in which items are stored indicating everything needed on the table for each meal.
- Label drawers with pictures if your children don't read yet. Use the inside of cabinet and closet doors to hang things. Draw the shape with a magic marker. Youngsters will enjoy putting things away! Older kids might not, but at least they can't say: "I didn't know where it goes!" (In some families these are the child's first words, before "Mama" and "Dada.") Keep a lightweight, easy, and safe step stool in a convenient place.
- Hang things on pegboards (on the insides of doors, if they offend you). Again, draw (or have an older child trace) the shapes.
- Keep delicate, dangerous, and the least used objects on the uppermost shelves. Reclaim the dead space above cabinets.
- Convert from hidden storage to up front and practical if space is at a premium. I entertain with a kitchen in the corner of my living room/dining area. No one seems to mind that everything shows.
- Take an informal survey. You'll discover, as I have, that people who use the Seal-A-Meal, blender, food processor, and crockpot keep them out and easily available.

- Buy a lazy-susan storage holder: everyone can see the potato peeler!
- Label drawers, cabinets, and doors. Color codes and pictures are handy until children learn to read.
- Think baskets: kids like to carry them. They are easier to use than trays for clearing the table.
- Keep paper goods handy if you can afford to buy them. If not, buy no-iron cloth napkins (on sale) and use them. Or buy a dozen cotton dish cloths (on sale) and use them in place of paper towels whenever possible.

Bedrooms

Have you ever noticed the number of items even a six-pound baby needs? The amount of stuff children accumulate multiplies each season, so try these ideas for easy bedrooms:

- Use the same set of sheets: wash, dry, and return them to the bed until they drop. Space in the linen closet is saved for other storage. You save money (if you pay for laundry). You save time folding, ironing, and putting away. Then when they are shabby you can buy new ones.
- Use different size straw baskets (in a corner) for hampers: separate white and dark or even items that need to be dry-cleaned.
- Think drawers whenever you buy a bed. I saved $100 by buying a platform bed with only two drawers rather than four. What a mistake! The two I have store out-of-season clothing; the others could have stored luggage or pillows or anything. Buy or build drawers under beds when your children get bedroom furniture. Build in closets (I love the new open plastic shelves) for upper/lower rods and for narrow shelf storage.
- Install opening doors (in place of sliding) because the backs of drawers hold a multitude of things.
- Install rods and shower curtain holders to hang

scarves/ties/ribbons/hats/gloves/sneakers on the inside of a door.

- Use hooks on doors or plastic cubbies (they are shaped like the top half of a "k") to store all kinds of things.
- Use a sleeping bag or comforter so your child can make the bed.

Think WALLS! Jeni once had a room full of stuffed animals. We finally tied each with a pretty satin ribbon and hung them from the walls. She loved it, and there was finally room to walk.

- Consider shelves up to the ceiling as headboards. (If money is no object, buy wall unit furniture that provides built-in storage.)
- Use crates, straw baskets, painted coffee tins, or shoe boxes and color-code them to store small objects.
- Create a well-lit desk space. Children need their own work center even when their work is coloring or pasting.
- Buy a file and use pictures or big numbers to divide folders.
- Post a bulletin board for display.

Some of the happiest and prettiest rooms reflect this motto: Think practical!

Idea #2: Organize for Easy Cleaning

Baths

- Keep supplies in a rack by the tub/shower if you want each bather to clean after using. Kids like to spray and scrub. Let them. Maybe it'll become a habit until they become "of age" and forget. Use bathroom hampers for towels.

- Use a paper towel dispenser in the bathroom if it isn't too expensive.
- Place a magazine rack on the wall.
- Create a vertical storage space behind the toilet to keep towels.
- Keep spare tissue rolls and boxes in each bath. Make it clear that the last served changes the roll. People with lots of spare time can worry about whether it rolls forward or backward; I care only that the last user puts the next roll on the holder.

Kitchen

- Keep cleaning supplies handy.
- Keep a small vacuum cleaner or dusters in or near the kitchen.

Everywhere Else

- Keep a mini glass wax dispenser near the mirror that smudges.
- Store supplies together in a carry basket.

In general, the easier it is to fetch and use, the more often it will be used to clean!

Idea #3: Organize Adult Space and Children's Space

I've been in houses where every place is kids' space, but I'm from the school of separate spaces. If your house is designed to have adult space and kid space, it is fairly easy to keep the former neat and clean by clearly defining your expectations. If you don't have separate space, your choices are to

- Make the child's bedroom his/her own playroom
- Create storage space in the adult space for children
- Let your child take over all the space

As a rule of thumb, the more space allotted the more needed, so choose accordingly.

- Think storage under the stairs. Some people build play houses or storage rooms; other use opening drawers in each step to store boots, bats, bundles, and more "stuff."
- Use a piece of furniture with doors to keep children's and adult's toys separate. (Bob once built a wall unit that had the TV, stereo, and bar on top and the children's storage on the bottom.)
- Use a linen closet as a storage closet for children's toys. (With sheets in bedroom and towels in bath, this is easy!)

> Think smiles. Shucking corn, stacking blocks, clearing the table, and wiping walls are happy times for those who make them so. The sooner the family learns to enjoy togetherness the better!

Idea #4: Organize for Safety

- Consider burglar alarms, window protection, and double-locked doors.
- Consider lights that go on automatically.

- Consider locks for

  liquor
  knives
  silver
  pills
  jewelry

- Practice fire drills.
- Post a list of directions: WHAT TO DO IN CASE OF . . .

Strangers:	Don't let them in. Don't say you're alone.
Fire:	Leave, then call fire department (get number from neighbors)
Medical emergency:	Call police. (They call ambulance.)
Emergency:	Call police
Telephone:	Never give name or information that parents are out or away!

IDEAS FOR PARENTS

Idea #1: Ten Commandments to Make Child Rearing Easier

These or your own individual standards shall be sacred convenants in thy household.

1. Thou shalt not say "yes" or "no" without considerable thought and spoken with care and affection.
2. Thou shalt not make major decisions without discussing with the other parent (or an adviser), especially if thy discussion might change thy decision.
3. Thou shalt stickest to thy "yes" or thy "no."
4. Thou shalt admit to mistakes openly and apologize for pain caused so that thou teachest thy children that to err is human and to be forgiving is good.
5. Thou shalt not permit verbal or physical abuse whither and with whomever thou goest. Thou wilt jeopardize thy serene future avoiding thy momentary embarrassment.

6. Thou shalt be loving, patient, generous, and sincere, but thou shalt not allow thy child(ren) to walketh over thy body.
7. Thou shalt deliver what thou promiseth and threaten only what thou shalt deliver.
8. Thou shalt develop fair expectations and maketh them clear and consistent.
9. Thou shalt not permit small children to get away with temper tantrums, nor middle-aged children to blackmail thee, nor senior children to drive thy car without permission.
10. Thou shalt acknowledge that if thou breaketh thy rules, thy teacheth thy children to breaketh them.

Idea #2: Let Go

Learn to let go early! Kiss, hug, say good-bye, and go! Whether you have to leave your loved one(s) to go to work, to enjoy private time, or to handle the business of life, eventually you will have to leave. Cutting the emotional umbilical cord is much harder for the mother than it is for the child, so it is best to start early to wean yourself with tiny little snips. Professional baby-sitters tell me that it is easiest for them, and apparently easiest for the child, if the mother separates when a baby is six to nine months old, though many mothers aren't yet ready to leave a baby that age with sitters.

Most of us want to avoid the all-too-common scene of the child clinging to a parent's leg, screaming while refusing to let go. Although each child reacts in an individual way, few children who learn early that separation is a natural event dependably followed by happy returns behave in an unpleasant "no-win" manner.

Life is a series of separations and reunions. Mother and child sever ties and begin new relationships starting with birth and continuing through life. Each commencement opens a new and healthy connection for the child with other people. Children soon learn that crying (if it is not unwittingly reinforced and rewarded) doesn't change the fact: whether they cry or not, a smiling Mommy will go away and return some hours later. Here are some ideas to help mothers prepare for the separations that occur naturally in life. Ideally, these separations should take place long before you leave for work.

Schedule a few hours a week just for you! Teach your children from the very start that personal care is a form of self-love, *not* selfishness.

- Enroll in a class: try the library, adult education, or a career seminar.
- Indulge in personal care: get a new hairstyle at a beauty school, get made up (free in a department store), exercise (run, jog, swim, bike), or join a class.
- Seek out friends: meet an old friend or make a new one to linger and chat with.
- Go shopping: enjoy looking, dreaming, and researching for future purchases.
- Start your job search and see what is out there.
- Stay private at home: learn to be "unavailable." Let the sitter take charge while you do whatever you wish alone and in private. Yes, it's OK to hire a sitter and lock the bedroom door. The key is not to open the door to plaintive little knocks.

Prepare to let go! Find a trustworthy mother-substitute. Exchange services for a few hours, if necessary. Use the information in the chapter on child care just as you would if you were leaving for school or work. Then practice the following routine:

- Leave excellent instructions.
- Kiss, hug, say bye-bye, then leave smiling. Do *not* hear the screams, do *not* turn back, do *not* hesitate, do *not* return to comfort. You must be in charge here! Manipulation is habit-forming, so you want to set a pleasant pattern. Smile,

leave, and find the nearest phone. Your child will probably be playing happily by the time you dial your own number.

- Call the sitter regularly if you are concerned.
- Don't leave your child asleep the first few times you go out. It may be easier for you, but it is hard to teach trust if you are deceptive. A child who goes to sleep and wakes up to a relative stranger will neither trust you not trust going to sleep. So even if leaving is difficult at first, remind yourself that honesty and trust are key ingredients to developing secure children.
- Return at a time the child understands. Little people don't relate to six o'clock but they understand a favorite program time or mealtime. They learn to trust from your dependability.
- Carry a small paper bag. Blow any guilt you may feel into it, then throw it away. Have a good day!

Prepare your child to let go! Just as you would prepare a child for a hospital visit (by reading books about the subject, talking about it openly, and taking the child to explore the hospital in advance), so you must prepare your youngster for the time you leave. Here are some ideas to help you help your child:

- Talk about it openly. Give reassurance that you will separate and return naturally.
- Take the child to visit the group care facility or the mother-substitute.
- Include the child as a participant in the interview and in the decision.
- Consider the child's feelings.
- Start out slowly by leaving your child for short periods of time.
- Don't sneak away. Confront your child's opposition openly but firmly.
- Present the information as a fact.
- Don't ask for or expect approval and don't pretend your child will love it when, indeed, your child might not.

- Read books, read magazines, see movies, and discuss TV shows before you go to work.
- Present a positive image about working mothers and their children.

Idea #3: Prescription for Cooperation

Sigmund Freud discussed the two most difficult jobs on earth: governing nations and parenting. Indeed, some working mothers manage both. But they usually wait until their parenting job is well done before they tackle nations. Since neither job has strict rules for success, we look for ideas and suggestions based on other people's advice and experience. We do this not because we trust in them implicitly but because they help us to define our job, to reinforce our own ideas, to make us aware of our own actions, and simply because we like to do our best at our most important tasks.

There is no perfect recipe to avoid parenting children who misbehave or "act out" just as there is no perfect recipe for avoiding cancer. Yet most of us accept the fact that we shouldn't smoke, drink alcohol, or coffee and that we should eat properly and exercise. Then, at least, even if we get cancer we can't blame it on our own negligence. So it is with parenting children. We try to learn the best way to raise them, and we hope for success. Then, even if it doesn't work, at least we can have the satisfaction of knowing that we tried our best. We try, too, to remember that acting out is a symptom of a problem and that we must focus on the problem causing the behavior rather than only on the symptomatic behavior. Look at acting out as if it were a fever. The fever is a symptom, a clue that announces a problem. We must focus on finding and treating the real problem, not only the symptom.

Here, then, is a prescription, not a magic formula, to help you deal with your children, to discipline them with love, and to cope with them if and when they do act out, while you try to focus on the purpose of the behavior and treat it.

Listen to what the children are saying! I must suggest that you consider your own special child as a primary source of information and clues. Listening is important in dealing with everyday situations, but it is absolutely imperative when dealing with traumas. One skill that is useful is to repeat the child's statement as a question. This elicits a more complete explanation.

Child: "Billy threw my books all over the place!"
Parent: "Billy threw your books all over the place?"
Child: "He threw my books down and kicked them."

Listening is an expression of the following truths:

- That you love them enough to listen
- That you care about their feelings
- That you can hear them without judging
- That you respect them

Avoid giving advice until it is requested! We love to give advice because we know better, have experience, and have dealt with similar problems. Kids don't like or listen to advice that is unsuitable, inappropriate, and ill-timed. Interruptions damage more than the advice helps. You are both better off if your child is upset with the problem, not with you. Remember, they need us to listen to and *acknowledge* their feelings, not to advise.

Learn the value of short and simple comments:

- "Really!" (stated with caring and concern)
- "I feel bad when you are
    a. angry"
    b. frustrated"
    c. upset"

- "I'm not sure I know what is best for you."
- "What do you think you can do to work things out?"

These words are your youngster's clue either to try to solve the problem independently or to ask for advice.

Ask them what they think:

- "How do you think *you* could solve the problem?"
- "How would *you* handle it?"
- "What are your options?"

Respect their right to say "no, thanks"! It is valuable for us not to intrude when a child prefers not to share information. We can offer to help, and they can refuse by saying "No, thanks." Let go for a bit, even though it hurts not to be needed and it is aggravating when they seek less qualified sources for advice. But so be it. They are struggling to assert their own strength and independence. And when we consider how we really want them to be when grown, we usually want them to be strong and independent.

Praise success but don't lecture:

- "I feel good when you do favors for friends."
- "I really enjoyed being with you today."
- "It was terrific to see you so happy."

Indicate your feelings without casting blame:

- "I get upset when I see a messy kitchen."
- "It makes me unhappy when you two are fighting."
- "I get angry when someone borrows my _____ without asking."

Use written notes to ask for things or complain (try to be funny!)

- "While you were out, the dog ate my shoe, barked, and cried because you didn't leave the bowl full."
- "Your school sent this note. What do you think we should do about it?"

- "Final warning! Scheduled attack on bedroom. Saturday 4 P.M. Everything in sight disappears."
- Make up or buy a list like the one below.

THINGS TO DO:

TO: ____________________
FROM: MOM
DATE: ____________

1. Make your bed
2. Eat breakfast
3. Brush your teeth
4. Don't forget pets
5. Empty dishwasher
6. Take out trash
7. Bring in pails
8. I'll be home at _____
9. 2 hours TV *max*!
10. *No* friends in house
11. Your friend _____ called
12. Practice the _____
13. Mow the lawn
14. Pick up the mess before _____ P.M.
15. I adore you!
16. I'm sorry I _____
17. Take out _____ from freezer
18. Don't eat _____. It's planned for dinner.
19. Call me at _____
20. PLEASE! No fighting!

Give youngsters a choice!
Toddlers:

- "Would you prefer peanut butter and jelly or cream cheese and jelly?"

- "Do you want to take a bath before or after this program?"
- "Do you want to wear the blue pants or the green ones?"
- "I see you are having trouble. How can I help?"

Elementary Age:

- "Do you want to do your homework after school or after dinner?"
- "Would you like to try day camp or sleep-away camp?"
- "What chores would you like to call your own?"
- "I see you are having trouble. How can I help?"

Preteens:

- "Which meals do you want to prepare?"
- "Do you want me to shop with you or meet you after you have finished?"
- "Would you like me to speak with the teacher or do you want to handle it yourself?"
- "I see you are having trouble. How can I help?"

WHY GIVE YOUNGSTERS A CHOICE?

- It teaches children from the youngest ages to be responsible decision makers.
- It helps them trust themselves and improves their self-esteem.
- It enhances a child's dignity.
- It makes life easier by avoiding the problem of the child saying, "No!"
- It makes specific commands more meaningful because of their infrequency.

Try to avoid being judgmental!
Say: "I feel good when you do well!"
Don't say: "You are good. . . ."

Give clearly defined expectations! Everyone needs clearly defined expectations. We expect a job description at work, students expect teachers to inform them of what they must do to pass, and children need to know what parents expect to ensure harmony. Give children lists and written directions to clarify rules.

Be consistent! Children learn to be consistent from parents who are consistent. If you, as a mother, change the rules to suit your convenience, your child learns from you how to do it. Inconsistency is called "sending mixed messages," and it both confuses people and makes them unnecessarily frustrated. Moreover, they never learn what is or is not acceptable behavior. Setting consistent limitations, so that your children know their boundaries, is one of the surest ways to avoid having children who act out.

Working mothers want to have harmonious relationships with their children. But harmony is achieved not by acquiescing but by having clearly defined parameters and by dealing with the transgressions decisively and consistently.

Idea #4: Prescription When They Don't Cooperate

This step-by-step technique works with children because it is fair and it shows caring and affection. I've noticed that even students who act out feel cared for and loved rather than angry when I use the "You're a terrific kid and I care about you but I cannot accept this behavior" approach.

If you, the busy working mother, make it your business to work through each stage consistently, your children will probably respond the way you want them to.

It is most important to stress that you should clearly separate the inappropriate action from the person. The person is not bad because he/she is doing something inappropriate. You should continue to make your child feel loved, adored, precious, and cherished and at the same time make him or her understand that such actions are not tolerated.

- *Occasion #1:* You inform the child (as if for the first time) that such and such action is totally inappropriate.
  SAY: "I will not accept this."
- *Occasion #2:* You express displeasure.
  SAY: "I feel bad that you did such and such. . . ."
  DON'T SAY: "You are bad." (Separate the action from the person.
- *Occasion #3:* Warn of ultimate consequences. Again, bring to the child's attention that the action is inappropriate and it is the last time you can let it go. Be specific: "I won't do this if you do that!" "You won't be allowed to do this if you do that."
- *Occasion #4:* Follow through consistently!

Idea #5: Discipline with Love

If a formula existed for "discipline with love" it might look something like this:

STROKE + STROKE + REPRIMAND + STROKE = DISCIPLINE WITH LOVE

Stroke:	"I love you."
Stroke:	"You're a very caring child."
Reprimand:	"You should not have hit your brother."
Stroke:	"I know you won't do that even when you get upset."
Discipline:	"If you disobey again, I won't allow you to go to the movies with your friends on Saturday."
Stroke:	"You're terrific."

Stroke:	"You're my best friend. I'm sorry you hurt."
Reprimand:	"I've been listening to your complaints for two days. I can listen for only another hour."
Stroke:	"You're such a nice person. I prefer being with you."
Discipline:	"If you continue complaining, I'll have to leave."

Idea #6: Withdraw Privileges

Withdrawing privileges has the advantage of changing children's behavior without damaging their psyche and, of course, without abusing them. In fact, most children not only respond well, they actually feel more loved and respect parents who mean what they say enough to withdraw the privilege. Deciding which privilege to withdraw is strictly personal and demands careful consideration. We must be certain

- To withdraw a privilege that is appropriate to the situation.
- To keep the time length of the punishment appropriate.
- To stick to it consistently.
- To temper justice with mercy.
- To choose a privilege that punishes the children, not the parents.
- To avoid the abuse of power.

Some Ideas of Privileges to Withdraw

Young children:

- Television: "If you do this again, you can't watch [title] this week." Withdrawing a favorite TV program, or even, as we've done, putting a lock on the TV from Sunday night to Thursday night, is a punishment that most youngsters respect. If you want the TV to keep your children entertained when you are not at home, decide which hours to turn it off when you are there to supervise.

- Going Places: "If you do this again you won't be able to go visit so-and-so with me."
- Fun time: "I can't play this game with a child who. . . ."
- Transportation: "I won't take you to . . . if you do this again, or if you don't do this." It is not fair to agree to take the child somewhere every week and then, in anger, change your mind. Now you're not withdrawing a privilege, you are not living up to an agreement.
- Being with: "If you keep this up you cannot stay in this room, office, car, store, party, movie."

Teens:

When you live with a teenager, the problems get bigger, but the punishments are fewer. These have been effective here:

- Grounding: Keeping the socialite "in" when the socialite wants "out" is very effective!
- Driving: Withdrawing driving privileges, or even chauffeuring ones, can be effective.
- Music: Is there a greater punishment than silencing a music box?
- Money: Until they pay for every movie, concert, and trip on their own, withdrawing paying for some of their considerable expenses works.

Considerable thought is necessary so that the punishment will teach the youngster a good lesson while not interfering too much with the working mother's life. Although you can't take away a summer program that cares for your child while you are working, there are still ample privileges that you can fairly and legitimately withdraw as children grow older. Of course, if you have terrific children who deal well with their responsibilities and handle themselves in a way that pleases you, you don't need to do this. But if your kids occasionally misbehave and are still learning to be responsible, it's a good idea to make up a list of privileges to withdraw when you need to use them.

LIST OF PRIVILEGES THAT MIGHT BE WITHDRAWN IF CHILD ACTS OUT

1.
2.
3.
4.
5.

Idea #7: Cope with Acting Out

When you're dealing with a discipline problem, and you are face to face with the child you love who is acting out ask yourself: "Would I accept this behavior if I were home twenty-four hours a day?" Chances are you wouldn't allow it. Working mothers sometimes give in because inside they feel guilty about leaving the child to go to work. Some are tempted to feel sorry for the child. They think: "It's not my child's fault, it's mine. He/she just needs more attention."

As a working mother, of course you want to give your child a lot of love and attention. But even if you can't give every-minute-of-the-day love, you can love your child enough to teach him/her appropriate behavioral expectations. You can also make clear just what behavior you are willing to accept. Most parents try to avoid raising rude or disruptive children because ultimately they will be responsible for their own behavior. Moreover, such children shatter family harmony.

Even when children act out for valid reasons, which you may or may not comprehend, the behavior is inappropriate and can't be permitted to continue. Since most children try acting out at one point or another, our task is clear. We must handle the situation so that they are not manipulating us. Then we have to look for the cause of the problem for which acting out is the symptom. This is especially relevant when the acting out interferes with our family and work.

The very expression acting out is scary because it brings to mind not only the variety of ways that children misbehave but also a picture of powerless parents.

Whether a toddler kicks, a third grader bullies, a sixth grader lies, an eighth grader steals, a teenager fails school or, worse, gets (someone) pregnant or is involved with drugs, parents suffer feelings of failure, frustration, guilt, and stress. Although most of us are able to accept and deal with our own children's problems (and thank our lucky stars that they aren't as bad as someone else's) those of us looking toward the future wonder and worry:

How would we handle it if our child acted out like that?

All that I have seen, read, and experienced indicates that the sooner we assert loving, but disciplined, authority the less likely it is that we will have to deal with serious problems. Parents who give in and give up when little children act out, or who forget that acting out is a symptom of a problem that needs to be dealt with, sometimes find themselves dealing with problems that they can't avoid later on. A long list of support groups such as Alanon or Tough Love help these parents, as do many school counselors and family therapists. I believe that it is best for children to learn this valuable lesson from us:

INAPPROPRIATE BEHAVIOR AT ANY AGE OR TIME IS NOT TOLERATED.

This book wasn't written to solve all acting out problems, but it will deal with one that working mothers fear: the tantrum.

Idea #8: Deal with a Temper Tantrum

Our offspring need love, stroking, praise, reassurance, and approval. They also need to know who is in charge. Whether you are experiencing the terrible twos, the traumatic twelves, or the terrifying twenties, it is uncomfortable at best, torturous at worst, to be in a no-win situation with your children.

Children need discipline in as large a dose as they need love. We know that. Therefore, it is important not to allow toddlers to be abusive. Experts recognize that during the terrible twos children stretch their limits and try to take charge.

It is easy to give in, to avoid hassles, and to pretend it doesn't matter, but parents should be aware that energy invested at this period shapes children's future behavior.

If tantrums are a recurring problem at any age, it is worthwhile to keep track of the patterns of this behavior. Keep a record of the date, time, and whatever stressful event might have provoked the tantrum. Be sure to consider what foods your child might have eaten or if he/she was hungry. Whether the cause is stress, frustration, or nutrition, you want to focus on solving the problem after you have calmed the behavioral symptom.

Let's consider the most typical tantrum that working mothers with young children confront (or fear).

The usual scenario shows mother and child at nursery school, in the store, or at a family gathering. Your child is making such a scene that you think everyone around assumes you are a child abuser. Anyone who has been "parent tested" by a toddler knows that an audience is required for this performance. You must accept that children are born both with an innate ability to test you and an amazingly instinctive sense of staging and timing. They not only know when and how to do it but also that their power increases in direct proportion to the number of onlookers.

Your child is screaming and moving his/her arms and legs with a strength you are sure you've never possessed. Your strained attempts to change the behavior are ignored. Believe me, mothers of all ages relate (and remember) your all-too-familiar rite of passage. But you must deal with it.

Assess whether your child is out of control:

- Is he/she hitting or kicking another person?
- Is his/her behavior hysterical?
- Has reasoning failed to change the behavior?

If you answered "yes," to all three questions, you can guarantee that your child is acting out in a temper tantrum. Here are some tactics to help you deal with this unfortunate experience.

Temper Tantrum Tactics

1. Talk soothingly and pick up and remove your child from the scene.
2. Take and leave him/her in a quiet space to calm down. Don't treat him/her to TV and don't provide toys or bribe with food. You are trying to show disapproval, not trying to reward the tantrum with fun, food, and games.
3. If the child hits *you* in a state of hysteria, making it impossible for you to remove him/her, try one of these strategies:
   - Move away, without participating, while your child continues the hysteria.
   - Wait out the hysteria while you pray that this is a singular event that will soon fade from memory.
   - Try holding the child down the way you do when a doctor gives a shot. Talk soothingly.

Remember, you can understand that your child is upset about the birth of a sibling, or about having to go to nursery school, or even because you wouldn't buy sugar-frosted cereal. You can sympathize or acknowledge the feelings, but you can't accept manipulative behavior. Like an addiction, it leads to more trouble and pain than you could ever expect.

Idea #9: Connect

All that I have learned reinforces the idea that connecting with feelings is one of the most important aspects of harmonious relationships. Learning to react to the child's *feelings* rather than to the words used to express them is a major step toward connecting.

- Scenario that connects
  Child: "I hate school. . . ."
  Parent: "Something must really be upsetting you."
- Scenario that disconnects
  Child: "I hate school. . . ."
  Parent: "Don't use the word 'hate'. Like it or hate it, you have to go."

Too often, we focus on the words and entirely miss the feelings being related. We also disconnect when we are so preoccupied with our own business that we don't have the time to listen.

- Scenario that connects
  Child: "Mom, Tommy knocked my books on the ground."
  Parent: "I feel bad that it is upsetting you."
- Scenario that disconnects
  Child: "Mom, Tommy knocked my books on the ground."
  Parent: "Tell me about it later, OK?"

These common disconnections occur so fast we don't even realize that we do them until the moment for sharing is lost: "Later . . ." and "I'm busy . . ." may be valid, but unfortunately children especially (but not exclusively) perceive those words to mean: "I don't care" or, worse, "Your problems aren't important!" Therefore, *how* you tell them that you can't listen to the whole story at that instant is extremely important. Your attention is warranted when they need it rather than when you are available to give it. Since we cannot always give it when they want it, it is even more imperative to connect to the feelings expressed regularly and consistently. Stating "I feel bad that you are upset" takes just a moment, but at least the child knows you care.

The following scenario illustrates connecting/disconnecting:
You want a household chore done.
They have plans for the moment and feel as busy as you do.
Your request is reasonable. *Their* cooperation could possibly depend upon how you connect to their feelings, so. . . .

- How to connect:
  Parent: "I need you to do this chore."
  Child: "But I'm busy. . . ."
  Parent: "I feel bad that you are busy but I have to ask you to fit this in. I can't possibly handle all of this myself."
- How to disconnect:
  Parent: "You must do this chore now."
  Child "But, Mom, I'm busy."
  Parent: "You're always too busy, why don't you ever. . . ."

Connecting doesn't always work, and it certainly cannot work if the person you are trying to connect with is already your enemy, but it is a technique that will eventually help. You can try the other alternatives, like yelling, crying, praying, denying privileges, and withdrawing services or waiting until they grow older and change or leave, but in the long run, connecting has advantages that none of these options offer. Those of us who want to connect but who already have set negative patterns to our listening must try to give up interrupting, advising, and problem solving. We must relearn how to listen in the special way that psychologists use that makes clients feel that their problems matter. The most important way to learn what is seriously troubling our children is to find out "where they are at." We can do that only by truly listening. Only then can we connect to their feelings.

We can pick up pointers to help us listen by paying attention to how the many radio psychologists do it. If you tune in to one of the radio talk shows featuring psychologists, you can listen to their callers' problems and pay attention to how the psychologists relate to their unidentified callers' emotional needs.

Learn Listening Techniques from Radio Psychologists

- Listen and acknowledge the problem with simple words that express caring and concern:
  "Really."
  "It sounds as if you are really troubled."
  "I know how hard that is. . . ."
- Restate the problem:
  "That's a real letdown/success/problem/bummer."
  "It sounds as if you are troubled/anxious/upset/thrilled."
- Restate the problem in the form of a question:
  "She yells at you all the time?"
- Explore, using the patient's/client's/child's own ideas to solve the problem by asking what efforts have already been made:
  "What have you done to try and solve this dilemma?"
- Then ask if the person would accept advice:
  "Would you want me to offer some ideas to help?"
- Offer the advice *if* the response is affirmative:
  "Perhaps, it would help if you. . . ."

We, as parents, must do our best to keep in touch with our children's emotional needs. Listening and connecting to them is the best advice I can offer.

Idea #10: Negotiate

We all recognize that fair expectations and reasonable requests rarely guarantee hoped-for results. This is as much a reality on the home front as it is in the marketplace. One part of the dilemma is the resistance of people to participating at the level we'd like; another part is that other people are so involved with their own problems that they neither see nor choose to relate to things from our vantage point.

We do, however, bring an important contributing factor to the bargaining table. We are sometimes so involved with solving a problem or taking care of whatever the business is that we unknowingly *disconnect* from the other person.

Concentrate on connecting: it's the key ingredient! Review Idea #9, "Connect," before starting negotiations. The skill of negotiating, like the skill of delegating, demands that you *connect* with another's feelings. We've each experienced turning people "off" when it is most important to turn them "on." This happens not because what we have to say is invalid but because *how* we say it disconnects. Once you have disconnected, failure is imminent, and you might as well leave the negotiating table, whether it is in a board room or the dining room. It sounds redundant, but connecting with feelings gives you more strength in negotiating than any of the rational reasons for your position.

Open negotiations. It is necessary to open negotiations without offending anyone. By talking "I" rather than "You," you take responsibility for your own statements and needs. You give others the dignity of feeling helpful and supportive of your needs without being burdened by being placed on the defensive. Say "I need" rather than "You must."

Listen to the other point of view. Give the others an opportunity to state their needs and sentiments fully. They see things only from their perspective, which is different from yours.

Acknowledge the other party's position. Simple statements like "I know this is difficult for you" or "I understand your position" are appreciated. At least you have the opportunity to state: "I recognize your position and I need you to understand mine."

"Save face!" However you phrase things while negotiating, it is important to allow the other party the common nicety of "saving face." Courtesy and generosity in giving in to requests on items that you can afford to relinquish lessen resentment. If you appear to be greedy or nonnegotiable of another's terms, you lose. At home, giving in to certain demands often implies allowing deserved privileges.

Don't apologize for legitimate requests. The oft-used beginning "I'm sorry but . . ." dooms you because it feeds the other's defense. After all, if you don't feel certain that your demand/request is justified, how can you convince someone else?

Strong bargaining positions sometimes appear weak. If there is no guarantee that the other party will give you what you want, even after a show of asssertiveness, you might as well avoid it. Losing after yelling your demands translates into a weak bargaining position. But if you say: "I can't . . ." you actually augment your position by appealing to another's ego. Often people need to feel helpful, even stronger. I'm not embarrassed to allow them to fulfill their ego needs while I fulfill mine.

Withdrawal of contributions. People sometimes don't appreciate your services until they have been withdrawn. If you find that you spend your time and energy giving to the person with whom you are negotiating, and you are not being successful, use the last resort: a cutback, a walkout, or a strike.

Even though it might be interpreted as manipulative or antifeminist rather than just plain human, here is my last negotiating strategy:

Cry. Crying is sometimes a real expression of emotional frustration. It is also an action that makes it easy for another person to respond positively. In some cases, it humanizes a woman who is perceived as too strong or too capable. But beware: many feel strongly that tears are a sign of weakness. To those individuals, it proves that a person, especially a woman, is incapable of trying to maintain both a home and a career. Therefore, keep in touch with your intellectual needs as well as your emotional ones.

If you think about one of the qualities that make successful career women, you will find this commonality: they speak softly and negotiate firmly!

Idea #11: Follow Your Hunches

If your life is as busy as I think it is, then it's unlikely that you'd have the time or energy to be suspicious unless you had a strong, nagging sensation that something was wrong. Your instincts are probably telling you something important. Follow your hunch and search. Find out the true story even if it means including the doctor, the school, or the sitter in your investigation.

There are, of course, some people who endlessly worry. They spend much time and expend an enormous amount of effort being concerned about things they can't control. Often, these people are preoccupied with "what if's" because they have been given the message that worry is a form of love.

Following your hunches helps everyone. It will temporarily allay fears if you discover that things are OK, and it justifies the rationale of worrying when things are not.

These Behavioral Changes Signal "Follow Your Hunch"

- Changes in patterns of eating, sleeping, going to regularly scheduled activities like play groups or, especially, school.
- New demonstrations of fearfulness, clinging, crying, withdrawing, or acting out.
- Sharp change in disposition from friendliness to withdrawal, or cheerfulness to hostility.
- Resistance to something that formerly was not a problem.

- Chronic problems in school or with friends.
- Avoiding one specific place or person.

How to Investigate the Problem

At any age, drastic behavioral changes indicate that something is wrong. Consider a physical checkup. Sometimes serious illnesses have been detected by parents who simply had a hunch that their child was behaving strangely.

Find a caring family practitioner. Although I used a fine pediatrician, if I had to do it again I'd find a family practitioner with an excellent reputation who would know the entire family history and would treat us all. Family practice practitioners, like internists and pediatricians, recommend specialists when the occasion warrants it. Teenagers feel uncomfortable in a waiting room with babies and often change doctors at the most sensitive time of their lives. Parents often find themselves describing a child's history to a newcomer at the very time they need the most support and advice.

Convenience is an important factor. Feeling free to discuss other family members' problems, after dealing with the one at hand, is both a timesaver and a support system most of us cherish. Because this specialty has reemerged in importance at the very time that medical careers have opened to more women, the ranks are filled with bright and caring doctors who are, or who hope to be, working mothers. I admit to a personal bias, confirmed by experience: they try to relate to our problems.

How to deal with the doctor.

- Speak to the doctor, in advance, if you are in a financial crisis. Generous doctors are rarely praised, but there are many of them.
- Ask for an appointment that fits into your schedule. The staff won't know when you are free or that losing time from work endangers your job security or income or that it could be detrimental to your child to miss school unless you inform them.

- Consider your own time and ask about it. If you know there is always a backup in the waiting room, discuss it with the doctor. Not all physicians are aware that such a problem exists. Some will help you to find the most convenient time or to be the first or last scheduled.
- Call before leaving home and ask if the doctor is on schedule. There is no use rushing if the staff knows that the doctor is delayed.
- Prepare for the waiting time effectively. Bring a book, write a letter, make lists.
- Encourage the child's father to participate. Doctor visits can be an intimate bonding time. Fathers who are uncomfortable in pediatric offices might be more willing to go with their children to their own family practitioner.
- Bring a specific list of symptoms; ask questions.
- Don't waste time worrying until *after* you hear bad news. You know it's unlikely, so why spend the energy?

Find out what's happening at school. If your child needs more help than you think is necessary, or appears to be doing less than you feel he/she should be, or has started to avoid school, don't wait: call or write to the teacher asking to discuss the matter. In late September or early October some teachers might not yet know your child. Don't let that stop you. Your initiating an interest will guarantee attention.

The answer to "How is my child doing in relationship to the class?" will give you clues as to what the problem might be. Passing test scores are irrelevant if your child isn't content. If the child is at the top of the class, ask: "Why do you think my child can't do the work alone?" or conversely "Should my child be doing homework at home?" or "Why do you suppose the work is so easy for my child?"

If the child is struggling to keep up with the work, you will want to know why the level of work is too hard. The answer could range from unusually high expectations on the part of the teacher, to unusually low contribution on the part of the student, to your child's inability to handle the work. It is not enough to know that the child isn't doing well. It is important to find out the reason.

When school life is a constant source of struggle, rather than of success, there is a problem somewhere. It could be with the staff, or the school, but it could also be a learning or an emotional problem. Some teachers volunteer information, but usually it is the parent's job to assess it.

To ensure everyone's peace of mind, and to pinpoint the problem, try these ideas:

- Discuss your child with the teacher and/or director.
- Schedule a medical checkup to find visual, aural, or nutritional problems or an illness.
- Have your child tested for learning dysfunctions. In some states, schools are required by law to test students upon written request by the parent. Don't be put off if your district discourages you. It is expensive, and some schools act more concerned with the cost than with the student. Likewise, some districts use tests that filter results so that minor dysfunctions don't show a discrepancy in learning achievement. Private testing services or consultation with psychologists (certified ones are sometimes covered by health insurance) are alternative sources.
- Find a support network through these personnel:
  School guidance personnel
  Private psychological services
  University or medical facilities
  State and local agencies
  Parent groups (ask for the names in your area)

Idea #12: Avoid Minor School Crises

One of the problems that children have to deal with when mother first starts working is learning to meet all of the school (substitute music, sport, club) responsibilities on their own.

Many children who usually remember everything get very upset on those few occasions when they do forget. Others, of course, have difficulty remembering anything.

One of my students once appeared to be having a mini-anxiety attack. She was an excellent student but had forgotten her homework two or three times in a short period of time. After class, I asked if she had a problem. She confided that her homework was missing because her mother had started working and couldn't bring it to school for her. Here she was, at fourteen, first beginning to cope with a lesson many of her friends had learned years earlier:

HOMEWORK BELONGS TO THE STUDENT, NOT THE PARENT!

But she was in a new, stressful situation, and she was reaching out to me for support. Because she was basically a responsible youngster, she soon learned to adjust to her new way of life. Some students, however, find it more difficult, especially if they have learned to rely on a mother who would run to school bearing lunch money, permission slips, and term papers whenever the phone rang with an urgent request. As much as I believe students have to learn to be responsible, I think we should help them avoid the anxious moments by appropriating the scouting motto: *Be prepared!*

Prepare a food care package. Prepare emergency food care packets together. They can be kept in children's desks or lockers. They should contain enough nourishing goodies to get the child through the occasional day when he/she forgets lunch or lunch money. Consider supplies that the child enjoys and that keep well: food bars, canned puddings, dried fruit, or nuts and juice will keep a child active.

Prepare a clothing care package. Suggest that your child pack a small bag with fresh underwear, pants, shirt, old sneakers, and gym clothes for occasions when snow, rain, a burst bladder, a bloody nose, or an unexpected period injures the spirit more than the body. The school nurse (whom you should always get to know) will help assure discretion.

Prepare an emergency cash envelope. Give your child enough cash either to buy lunch, pay for a ride home, or pay for dues. Be clear that if emergency funds are spent recklessly they must be replaced from the child's allowance or earnings. If crime is a problem, ask a staff member to hold the money. Office staff can be as helpful as teachers.

Find an emergency contact person. Most schools require the name and phone number of a person who can go to school to pick up a sick child in medical emergencies if parents are unavailable. Your children might need to be able to call someone for less drastic situations. Give them clearly defined parameters of acceptable (and unacceptable) circumstances so they call that person for legitimate reasons.

Teach kids that school belongs to them. It's one thing to be supportive when children occasionally forget; it is quite another to cripple them into chronic dependency. Ultimately, the children bear the final responsibility for schoolwork, and the best way we can prepare them for it is to give them responsibilities. Try though we do, it is sometimes only the really tough lessons like failing gym because they are chronically unprepared (forgetting gym clothes is the usual reason), missing a field trip because they forgot the money, or having to work to pay for a lost item that teach our children that responsibilities belong only to them. These lessons serve their purpose well.

Idea #13: What You Can Do to Help Your Child's Father Be "Daddy"

In our household Daddy is on a pedestal, and his three daughters continue to adore him as they grow into womanhood. I think the best thing I do to contribute to their relationship is to let them enjoy it without my interference. This may sound easy but, actually, it is hard not to stay involved in everything. Here's how:

- Encourage father-child time alone. If you expect the father and the child to have intimate bonds, they have to create them separately. Shopping, doing errands, making visits to the doctor, and having breakfast out together can be as much fun as going to the zoo or the ball game.
- Encourage children to take nonsexist roles. Encourage interested daughters to hang out with Daddy at the shop, on the boat, or at the ballfield. Encourage fathers to introduce their sons to the dry-cleaner and the laundromat as well as the kitchen. Together, they'll probably enjoy these activities.
- Encourage independence. If they go fishing and forget about planning lunch, they'll come home giggling about the Milky Ways and Coke they bought at a vending machine.
- If you feel jealous of the stong bond between them, remember how lucky they are to have each other and you are to have a participating poppa in your life.

WHAT TO DO WHEN ALL ELSE FAILS

This book offers a lot of sound advice, and it illustrates many ways in which working mothers have managed successful households. But if you think that I think this means that we'll all enjoy mess-free living and tidy homes forevermore, don't believe it! No book, even one chock-full of good ideas, can convert those who refuse to cooperate or those who are forever slobby. What it can do is provide you with support so that you can begin to live a life in which you don't do it all. Here are some final strategies to consider for those rough times.

Idea #1: Make a Contract

While looking through my files, I found some letters, contracts, and threats made to my youngest daughter, now grown up, who did not always meet her responsibilities. With her permission, I've included them as a way to try to help other mothers get their children to do their chores. By the way, even if the dishwasher is sometimes still full when I want to load it, or the garbage pails are left on the street, the same forgetful child would never dream of asking me for socks or a clean blouse. When she needs something ironed, she does it. When she prefers to eat earlier than my husband and I do, she prepares her own meal. So, in an offer to show you a healthy, nondestructive way to get your children to cooperate, Jenifer and I are sharing some of our private correspondence. When I'm upset, I often write lengthy letters expressing what I don't like. It relieves me of my anger. Ninety-five percent of the time I have the good sense to rip them up. Contracts, on the other hand, rarely offend anyone.

Psychologists and teachers as well as parents agree that sometimes children need contracts. To see their chores written down or even to keep charts with stars and smiling faces helps motivate them. Visual aids help at school, in business, in political campaigns, and at home!

As you will notice, I am not above using money or "bribery" to get certain things done. In school I offer "educational motivation" for extra credit. At home, I offer privileges or money. It's the capitalist system, and I agree with it. I feel people should learn young to earn what they want. Not everyone agrees!

Dear Jenifer,
Only you can take responsibility for your life. I'm concerned about the following:

NUTRITION:

You need protein for breakfast, lunch, and dinner. I will withdraw after-school "junk" food (from fast-food restaurants) and snacks unless you take care of your proper nourishment.

STUDYING:

When your schoolwork is undone, only you are unhappy. We've locked the television after school and expect you to do your schoolwork. We will provide tutors, help, and supervision, but you must provide effort. Your reward or punishment will be how *you* feel at school, when you are in class.

HOUSEHOLD:

1. Your room/laundry are your responsibilities.
2. Your animals belong to you.
3. In the kitchen you must set/clear table.
4. Garbage pails out/in.

Please do your best. A treat will be waiting.
Love,
Mommy

Parent/Child Contract

These are your responsibilities in the household:

1. Empty dishwasher
2. Set table, clear table
3. Take out garbage Monday A.M.–Thursday, A.M.
4. Bring in pails Monday and Thursday
5. Your laundry
6. Police the lawn Saturday

These are your responsibilities for your pets:

1. They must be fed
2. They need water
3. Announce in advance when they are running out of food
4. Change litter
5. Use the pooper scooper!!!

These are your privileges:

1. Television on weekends
2. Telephone privileges
3. Guest privileges
4. Social and sport activities
5. Extra magazines and clothes

These are the conditions:

IF YOU DON'T MEET YOUR RESPONSIBILITIES, I'LL WITHDRAW PRIVILEGES!

Bribery Clause:

You'll get a $2.00 bonus if everything is done!

____________________ ____________________

Irvina Lew Jenifer Lew

Idea #2: Make a "Pick-up Time and Date"

My friend's mother kept an extremely tidy house. Her children paid a steep price for leaving things lying around. Whether it was a schoolbook, a pair of mittens, or an all-important piece of jewelry, the item disappeared. Her mother knew nothing about it when asked. Yet some months later the object would reappear, as mysteriously as it had disappeared, on the front hall table.

Yes, I think this is cruel, and I could never do it. I'm the wife who refused to let her husband throw out toys left in the yard because I thought it was a mean trick. Needless to say, however, my family leaves things around, and my friend's family does not.

In a search for a benign solution to the common problem of what to do when people leave things thrown around, I suggest the following activity:

- Post the word and tell everyone a day or hours in advance that at a specific date and time anything left around the house will be collected. Some households can plan a regular "pick-up time" such as before a family meal or a family meeting: "Now hear this. At five o'clock on Sunday, May

3rd, any item left in the mutual rooms (living, kitchen, den, baths, hall, garage, terrace, yard) will be collected." (If private rooms, such as bedrooms, are included give extra time or specify clearly.)

- Create a time and place when the item can be bought back. Each person can pay by doing an extra household chore or performing a service.

Idea #3: Go on Strike

I'm tame compared to other mothers. Recently, when asked what a mother should do when all else fails, I replied: "If your family situation makes it impossible to sit down and discuss things, or to delegate chores effectively, you might have to take drastic action." But the drastic action I recommended was mild indeed. I suggested tht the mother manipulate the family into cooperation by taking to her bed for a weekend or longer if possible. That way, the family would manage to survive without the mother meeting everyone else's needs. I added that at the end of her ailment she should commend the family for being so capable and insist that the reason for her "headache" was because the family needs are so great that she alone can't manage them. Knowing how capable they are (she should continue) reassures her that she won't need to do everything for them. After all, her health and well-being are important to the whole group.

Well, I'm mild—conniving perhaps, but tame. A woman whose idea received national notoriety was recently the subject of newspaper articles. Her frustration led her to a far more drastic, and probably more effective, idea. She went on strike! As *Newsday* reported, she got so frustrated that she threw her eighteen-year-old's laundry out on the front porch and sat down under a big sign that said STRIKE!

She refused to prepare meals until everyone agreed to cooperate. What is more, the article indicated that now the family "hostility level" has decreased and that the entire group meets to discuss who does what chore. A family team surfaced after the effective strike. And to give you an idea of how far-reaching and universal the problem is, Phil Donohue invited her to discuss the solution to her problem on his popular television show.

Who knows if the price tag is worth it for you? After all, her husband could have walked out, the kids could have left, and she might have been alone. Nevertheless, it's an idea to consider when all else fails.

Ideas When All Else Fails

- Get into bed saying you have a severe problem and stay there. It is doubtful that anything will get done *your* way, but your family will survive.
- Work late, take a class, or schedule a business trip.
- Try to plan to go away for a while.
  a. Visit a friend you haven't seen since high school.
  b. Visit a relative.
  c. Arrange a business trip.
  d. Take a course (for a week or three) at an out-of-town campus.

If you can get away, the family will make do and appreciate you more. When you return from your trip, your bed, or even your once-a-week night out, make sure to follow up with the following ideas:

- Stroke them! Applaud everyone whose cooperation helped the family to survive. Make your husband, sitter, children, or mother-in-law feel that you never could have managed without them.
- Let go! Don't go back to doing everything for them!
- Be as loving as possible! Reassure them of your love. Let them know that their ability to be independent makes you feel like a successful mother of wonderful children.

Dear Reader,

I do hope that this book has met your needs and given you the support and information necessary to help you with some of your most difficult dilemmas. Although no book can guarantee cooperation from those who refuse it or neatness from those won't try it, what it can do—and what I hope it has done—is to show appreciation for the effort and the considerable talents that each of us contributes when we combine the worlds of homemaker and wage earner.

I would love to keep in touch and to hear about your own ideas that work as well as those that you used as a result of reading this book. Good luck and please write!

Irvina Siegel Lew
c/o Atheneum Publishers
115 Fifth Avenue
New York, N.Y. 10003

APPENDIXES

APPENDIX 1
GLOSSARY OF CHILD CARE TERMINOLOGY

This glossary is designed to introduce the vocabulary used to describe child caregivers because the more commonplace the usage the more words are needed to talk about it. Mothers have always used helpers to supplement parental love and attention. Now they have programs as well. So I've defined the differences and interpreted the nuances of meanings of the many words we use for child caregivers in and out of the home.

In-Home Helpers

These definitions are based on personal experience with many different child caregivers. Of the ones mentioned, our family has hired all but two: we could never afford (nor dare to bring) a governess to our humble home, and we have not yet enjoyed the company of a houseboy. (I'm hoping for one of those now more than ever!)

AU PAIR: Originally, a young foreigner who performed child care duties and a few light housekeeping ones in exchange for the chance to live in another country. A tiny salary supplemented room and board. Today, people seek au pairs at specialized agencies and in newspaper advertisements. Today, they include farm girls who wish to summer at the beach or live in big cities and all types of interesting people searching for a change of scenery. Au pair help is, by its very nature, temporary and is not ideal if you are looking for a long-term commitment.

BABY-SITTER: This word implies a job description that includes a lot of love, little pay, and limited, if any, housework. It could be a sixteen- or sixty-year-old neighbor paid at an hourly/daily/weekly rate to adore your child(ren). Increasingly, baby-sitters are male as well as female. They rarely live in but are ideal for the before or after school hours.

CAREGIVER: A person charged with the responsibility of caring for a child. This term could be used for anyone from the professionally certified nursery school teacher to the baby-sitter who lives next door. It is a generalization and can refer to men as well as women.

GOVERNESS: Usually a person trained to care for children and to teach manners and proper speech. I've never heard of a governess who did housework.

HOUSEBOY: I wish I had firsthand experience with houseboys because the ones I've met clean, cook, arrange flowers, serve, and keep swimming pools pretty. Unfortunately, my lifestyle doesn't call for that kind of help! Although some houseboys care for children, it is not their major role. Men called "sitters" or "big brothers" care for children, but they don't often do housework.

HOUSEKEEPER: A person who manages the household while caring for the children. The employer makes the priorities clear during an interview. In addition to caring for the children, housekeeping responsibilities include cooking, ironing, cleaning, taking messages, paying delivery people, and tasks we think of when we say: "I wish I had a wife!!!"

MAID: A person whose primary charge is housekeeping duties and also cares for the children. This word, even when it was commonly used, had a derogatory connotation. To many people it is an offensive, negative term. Like the difference between janitor and custodian, maids and housekeepers do similar work, but the latter expresses it in a nicer way and is regarded as more appropriate.

MOTHER'S HELPER: Mother's helpers are like local au pairs. They are usually young, enjoy being with children, and rarely do much housework. Some live in for weekends, summers, or even the school year. Students work their schedule around yours (if you are lucky) in exchange for room, board, and a small salary.

MOTHER-SUBSTITUTE: This is your alter ego, the one steady person who takes your place while you are working. Housekeeping is decidedly second place to child rearing. In fact, mother-substitutes don't usually clean. You can find mother-substitutes willing to do some household chores if you specifically request it and discuss what they are willing to do. They are likely to be relatives, neighbors, friends, or retired people in the community who choose to work at home (yours or theirs) rather than in unfamiliar territory.

NANNY OR NURSE: This is a person trained as a child-care professional. They usualy live in and rarely do household chores. Some are trained as practical nurses and specialize in infant care.

Out-of-Home Family Care

It is a tribute to the parents who have had to create individual options and to those entrepreneurial ones who have filled the need that there are so many varieties of child care. They range from the typical informal arrangements with a neighborhood sitter, to strictly regulated and licensed facilities, to new an innovative solutions. Let's distinguish the differences between them.

COOPERATIVE CHILD-CARE GROUPS: This category includes a small group of children with or without one paid staff member.

About ten children meet in a facility or in each family's home. Parents (or, occasionally, a mother-substitute) rotate as staff members to cut down the expense and increase involvement.

COOPERATIVE CHILD-CARE SERVICES: Parents, particularly those who live in a tightly knit community such as a housing development, apartment complex, or campus, form their own personal cooperative venture. They use "chits" as payment for each hour of baby-sitting service from another member of the group. The children go to another parent's home, and often they go to a friend's home and the same friend comes to their's. Each group organizes bookkeeping in its own way, but often one individual at a time is responsible. This is a wonderfully inexpensive solution for those who can afford to give as well as receive the service and, because peers form the group, it is fairly easy to find good people to sit.

EMPLOYER-SPONSORED DAY CARE: In early research for this book I found the following quote in the *New York Times:* "Companies have their pens poised now, where they used to have their hearing aids turned off. . . . Today, both men and women want to parent and the corporation that wants the best, must have a recognition of individual needs." Perhaps, but those pens once poised in good intentions have been so busy slashing funding (and jobs) during the economic crunch and a political era that put women's needs at the bottom of the list that day care hasn't improved to any impressive extent. Parents have to search to find the few corporations that provide day care. Some charge an hourly fee as high as the minimum wage. But hope is on the way! Politicians use day care as a campaign issue, and Congress has proposed tax incentives to companies that sponsor day care.

GROUP CARE IN A SITTER'S HOME: This is the most typical form of child care in the United States today. Your children, along with four or five others, have a second home and a play group of peers and are supervised and cared for by one devoted individual. Usually, parents and children are comfortably secure with the arrangement and everyone profits. But when one of my fourteen-year-old students and her fifteen-year-old sister once stayed home from school for a week, I asked why. She replied, "My mother went away and we had to watch the little brats."

This was, to be sure, a rare occurrence, but I wouldn't want one of your children cared for by two teenagers while their mother, your sitter, went away. It reminds us all to ask the sitter, "Who cares for the children when *you* are sick or otherwise unable to be there?" and to be sure and go inside to check things out regularly.

INDIVIDUALIZED CARE IN A PRIVATE HOME: The child's second home is often with a family member, friend, or neighbor. Usually, your child is the one special playmate for the sitter's child.

LICENSED GROUP CARE: Many communities require regulations and licenses to ensure safety and to guarantee minimum standards, although church-sponsored programs and those that involve fewer than seven or ten children are often exempt. Licensing alone doesn't ensure that the program is good because enforcement is spotty, regulations often concern seemingly trivial matters like square footage of floor space, fenced yards, and number of toilet facilities. Yet it does provide the parent with certain safety assurances and usually guarantees that the provider has some training or credentials in child care. Parents can work toward achieving better-trained personnel, more regulations, stricter enforcement, and quality control supported by accreditation.

PRIVATE NONPROFIT DAY CARE: Charitable, social, and religious organizations often provide child care services at a reasonable cost. Many parents feel more comfortable sending their children to church-sponsored programs not only because of the lower cost but also because they recognize that the personnel, often trained, skilled volunteers, are working because they love children.

PRIVATE PROPRIETARY DAY CARE: These programs are private enterprise for profit. They range from Mom and Pop homes, to small nurseries, to chains of professionally managed, franchised child care centers. Some are highly regarded, and most have their own particular philosophy with which you should familiarize yourself.

PUBLICLY FUNDED DAY CARE: Publicly sponsored day care is regulated by government, staffed by accredited directors and usually by trained employees, and provides a desperately needed service at minimal or no cost. Children usually come from families that meet specific criteria, though occasionally, if a slot is available, other children will be accepted. The mother who works for a minimum wage and has to pay for child care to support herself and her family is most in need of a supportive day care system. One woman who applied for day care had to show notarized letters from her employers (as a domestic worker she had to show five letters guaranteeing her wage), and she had to show proof of her children's Social Security numbers before they could enroll. Although the red tape (see the section on AFDC, page 15) is frustrating, the services provided will assure her children of excellent care while she begins to assume the giant task of surviving as a single mother. Increasingly, day care has been a compaign issue, but rarely do the candidates who propose it win the election. As the parents' vote becomes louder and women's activism grows stronger, these needs will surely have to be met.

WORKPLACE CARE IS A HOME OFFICE: More and more individuals have created home office space. Increasingly, with computer operations perfomed in the home, employed personnel spend some of their work days at home and others in the office. One couple arranges its work weeks so that he is home on Monday and she is home on Friday. Thus they cut down their baby-sitting expenses and spend more time with their first child.

Among the countless people who now work in home offices are accountants, beauticians, bookkeepers, computer operators, cosmetologists, doctors, lawyers, sales personnel, mail order proprietors, secretaries, teachers, writers, and, of course, the sitters who tend to our children.

In addition, entrepreneurial moms have created thousands of cottage industries in an effort to bypass the rigid confines of a nine-to-five schedule. These ranks are populated by some who have become millionaires and who are featured in women's magazines as the women who have managed to be there with their children while creating successful businesses. I have spoken with women who tell me that their at-home office personnel are as comfortable answering mail as they are warming a bottle. We used to hear about women who brought their babies to the office (but this became increasingly difficult as babies became toddlers). Then we became used to the idea of the workplace in the home. Now we read about a new innovation: one professional mother, who felt it wasn't feasible to work from home, leased a small office in her office building and staffed it with a mother-substitute, decorated it with toys and play equipment, and shared the operating expenses with mothers who work nearby.

The plentiful options and abundant alternatives provide children with care that lovingly supplements the family's. In spite of the problems, thousands of homes and facilities are staffed with loving people giving our children care, affection, and safety while supplementing their education. Determining which best suits your needs depends not only on your priorities and limitations but on the most important factor of all: in-depth parental evaluation of the child caregiver.

Then, after you have made the best child care choice, you still have to consider the contingencies and plan on arranging for substitutes (or backup strategies) for days when you or your child or the caregiver or your child's father is sick! Don't worry, though, you'll handle it. We all do!!

APPENDIX 2
LEGAL RESPONSIBILITIES TO HOUSEHOLD EMPLOYEES*

Legal responsibilities to the people who care for our children are clearly defined. Many working mothers/employers have ambivalent feelings about meeting these legal criteria: on the one hand, they are reluctant to deal with what is considered a costly nuisance, and, on the other hand, they are aware of the moral and legal responsibilities to those who care for our children. It is a most important job, yet it is often underpaid and underrecognized. Additional recent legal changes augment the status of domestic workers and assure that these workers, often the lowest-paid segment of the working mother population, get some of the benefits that the rest of us take for granted. Problems occur because many, if not most, household employees request to be paid "off the books" because they want and need to bring home the maximum earnings. The temptation to pay that way because it is less complicated and less costly is great. But I would be amiss if I didn't tell you about the risks in-

*The information for this chapter comes from Internal Revenue Service, *Child and Disabled Dependent Care,* Publication 503 (rev. November 1983).

volved. Again, I suggest you come to terms with this question before you hire someone to care for your children.

Social Security Regulations

If you pay a household worker $50 or more during a calendar quarter, you must file Form 942, Employer's Quarterly Tax Return for Household Employees, to remit FICA taxes.

You must file an annual W-2 form with the Social Security office showing the wages and the Social Security tax paid. In late 1984, your share of the tax was 7 percent and the employee's share was 6.7 percent of the first $37,800 of wages paid. In 1985, the employee's share increased to 7 percent and the wage base increased to an as yet undetermined figure.

You must give a copy of the W-2 form to your employee.

Legal Consequences and Problems

It is uncommon, but possible, for household workers who choose not to declare an income while working for you to apply for Social Security benefits at a later date. To prove their work experience, they might report the time they spent in your employ. Should this occur, it is possible that the Social Security office will turn the case over to the Internal Revenue Service, which may try to collect back taxes from you.

You can plead ignorance of the law, but if the Internal Revenue Service chooses to proceed to the maximum of the law, the penalties are staggering. It can legally collect from the employer not only the taxes you should have paid but also those the employee should have paid, plus interest (currently 11 percent) and late charges. The late charges are calculated as follows: a maximum of 5 percent for the first five months and a maximum of .5 percent for the next forty-five months, to a total maximum of 50 percent.

Consider this atypical, but true, instance reported by Tamar Lewin in the *New York Times* on March 2, 1984: an employer of an illegal alien had to pay $2,000 in back Social Security taxes, plus interest and fees, which came to about another $2,000.

Although few individuals actually get caught by the IRS and have to pay monies due, there are two situations which are more likely than others to cause an employer to be caught:

- Illegal aliens who apply for legal status (a green card) tell the authorities that they have already been working in the country. At the same time that this supports their case for legal green cards, it places the employer in a very expensive position to pay past due taxes, when, and if, the IRS comes to collect.
- Workers who decide to accumulate enough Social Security credits so that they can retire with benefits are also apt to report the years they worked in your employ.

Federal Unemployment Tax (FUTA)

You are liable for FUTA tax for any employees to whom you pay wages of $1,000 or more in a calendar quarter in the current or preceding year.

For 1983 and 1984 you are required to pay a federal unemployment tax at 3.5 percent of the first $7,000 of the employee's annual wages. In 1985, the rate increased to 6.2 percent.

Some states require that you pay a state unemployment tax as well, in which case a portion of the state tax will be credited toward the federal requirement. Contact the Unemployment Division in your state's Department of Labor to get the correct forms and specific amounts. Form 940, Employer's Annual Federal Unemployment (FUTA) Tax Return, is designed to take applicable state credits into account.

Disability Aid to Full-Time Domestic Workers

According to an article by Susan Chira in the *New York Times* on May 5, 1983, a few states, including New York, New Jersey, Rhode Island, Hawaii, California, and the Commonwealth of Puerto Rico, have passed laws requiring employers of full-time domestic workers (forty hours a week) "to provide salary insurance for disabilities suffered by the employees off-the-job. . . . Employers will not be required to pay health insurance or medical costs in the case of an off-the-job injury or illness."

The insurance, costing between $50 and $100 a year, protects the employer from being sued by the employee.

Insurance: Homeowner and Health Care

Workers compensation benefits to provide benefits for a worker hurt on the job. "Employers of domestic workers, as well as most workers in the state, must now pay worker's compensation benefits when an employee is hurt on the job. The benefits are set at two-thirds of an employee's weekly salary, not to exceed $125 a week. There is no time limit on benefit."*

Homeowners insurance to provide coverage in case of an on-the-job injury to a domestic worker.

Health insurance, if you are associated with a health plan in which your employee can become a part, or can provide one. You will find that this is an incentive to a domestic worker just as it is to any other.

There is so much to consider when you are seeking the best care for your children that it is easy to dismiss legal and technical details by focusing on lovingness, caringness, safety, and reliability. But all of this information is valid to every working mother who employs help.

Ideally, you should discuss these legal and financial matters

*The *New York Times,* May 5, 1983, Susan Chira (B3).

with an expert before you start interviewing. Then take them into consideration before finally hiring a domestic worker. The truth is that when you hire help at home you are an employer even if you leave home to be an employee. I've no doubt you can handle the former job as well as the latter!

APPENDIX 3
TAX CREDIT FOR CHILD CARE EXPENSES

This section is designed to lead you to the source* and to clarify some basic questions about the tax credits available to working parents who pay for child care. It will illustrate how a few typical families use their tax credits to compensate for the expense of child care. Then it will give you some ideas of what you cannot do if you want to avoid being challenged by the IRS.

Since individual circumstances differ to a vast degree and the law changes constantly, your personal tax professionals are the ones to advise you on your particular situation. Remember, I'm the one who says

YOU CAN'T DO IT ALL!

This is one instance when you shouldn't even try. The idea of leaving the tax work to the professionals is a solid one. Besides, the cost of preparing your tax returns can be deducted on your next year's returns if you itemize your deductions.

*The information in this section is from Internal Revenue Service, *Child and Disabled Dependent Care,* Publication 503 (rev. November 1983). The bulletin includes filled-in forms 940, W-2, and W-3.

How do I claim tax credit for child care? You must file your return on Form 1040 or Form 1040A, *not* 1040EZ, and attach Form 2441, which is called "Credit for Child and Dependent Care Expenses." Married couples living together must file a joint return. If you are divorced, legally separated, or married but living apart, study the section called "Marital Status" to see if you can file separately and qualify.

What is a tax credit? Tax credits are dollars subtracted directly from the total amount of taxes due. But you can't subtract more than you owe. The IRS won't make refunds if your child care credit is greater than your tax liability.

How do tax deductions differ from tax credits? Tax deductions are deducted from your income before you calculate how much taxes you owe. Tax credits are worth more because they are subtracted at the end, from the amount you must pay.

What are the eligibility requirements? The government has a long list of eligibility requirements, and some are very complicated. Each one is written to apply to specific situations, so find a professional or study hard. This primer will give you an idea of some, but not all, of the factors involved:

- *HOME UPKEEP* If you provide more than half the cost of running your household, you are keeping up a home. So, if you live with another family, or are supported by AFDC, or have a former husband contributing to home upkeep, be sure you have accurate records of how much you contribute.
- *WORK REQUIREMENTS* You and, if married, your spouse, must work or actively look for work or be a full-time student with an employed spouse during the calendar year for which you are taking the credit.
- *QUALIFYING PERSON* Dependents under fifteen, disabled dependents, and spouses qualify. If you are divorced, your child does not have to be your dependent to qualify if you have custody for a longer time than the other parent.
- *ELIGIBLE WORK-RELATED EXPENSES* These are the expenses for care of the qualifying person that allowed you

(and your spouse) to work. These expenses must have been for the well-being of the qualifying person and can include housekeeping, room and board costs (not tuition), and group care if the primary purpose is for you to work.

How do I figure out my tax credits? The tax credit is based upon a percentage, according to your adjusted gross income, of your actual care expenses (be sure to save all of your expense receipts for four years!) to a maximum allowable expense of $2,400 for one dependent and $4,800 for two or more dependents.

These percentages range from a maximum of 30 percent to a minimum of 20 percent of the maximum allowable expense for child care or, if it is less, the earned income of the lower earning spouse. You cannot claim greater expense than the least income! For example, if your adjusted gross income is $10,000 or less, your tax credit is calculated as follows:

for one dependent: $2,400 × .30 = $720
for two or more dependents: $4,800 × .30 = $1,440

If your gross income exceeds $28,000, you can claim
$2,400 × .20 = $480
$4,800 × .20 = $960

The 30 percent of $2,400 or $4,800 maximum allowable expense is reduced by 1 percent for every $2,000 of income above $10,000. The reduction stops at incomes above $28,000 at 20 percent of the maximum allowable expense. Here's the 1983 chart:

ADJUSTED GROSS INCOME		APPLICABLE PERCENTAGE
OVER	BUT NOT OVER	
$0	$10,000	30%
10,000	12,000	29
12,000	14,000	28
14,000	16,000	27
16,000	18,000	26

ADJUSTED GROSS INCOME		APPLICABLE PERCENTAGE
OVER	BUT NOT OVER	
18,000	20,000	25
20,000	22,000	24
22,000	24,000	23
24,000	26,000	22
26,000	28,000	21
28,000	and over	20

Sheila and Dave

Sheila and Dave are the typical American couple, according to United States Bureau of Census figures. Dave earns what the U.S. Bureau of Census says is the average income for men: $20,870. Sheila earns the average wage of the 27.7 million working wives in the United States: $8,600.

Their child care expenses are high because they pay a nursery school and a college student who baby-sits before and after school. During the summer and on school vacations she serves as a one-person camp leader and takes the children swimming and to the library ($100 per week). Sheila has been criticized for working for nothing, but she sees it differently. She feels she would have to live just as modestly on one income, but this way she foresees a more comfortable future. Besides, she enjoys working.

Although their combined income is $29,470, they reduce their adjusted gross income to $25,860 in the following ways: They contribute $2,000 to an IRA fund. Dave, a salesperson, uses his car for work and claims an employee's business expense deduction of $750. They also claim the deduction for married couples when both work: 10 percent of the lower-paid spouse's earned income: $860. This brings their adjusted gross income down to $25,860. Sheila and Dave spend the maximum child-care expense of $4,800. They claim a credit of 22 percent or $1,056.

Lisette

Lisette is a single parent, who until recently was supported by Social Services. Her monthly income of $400 included her former husband's weekly child support, which he paid directly to Social Services. Although Lisette paid a neighbor to care for her preschool child while she attended classes, she wasn't eligible to claim tax credits because Social Services provided for more than half of her upkeep.

As soon as Lisette graduated from a local community college, she was able to get a job starting at $200 a week. Lisette is eligible to claim the maximum credit for one child, but it is still difficult for her to make ends meet. Nevertheless, although she doesn't earn great deal more than what the U.S. Department of Labor defines as the poverty level ($9,000) and can barely manage to pay $50 a week for child care, she is confident she will survive. She expects things to improve drastically next year: her child will be enrolled in full day kindergarten and she is promised a raise. Lisette is so thrilled to be free of welfare and on the road to success that she knows she can make do until then. For her, the tax credit has been a substantial help.

Betty and John

Betty and John have three school-age children. He's a schoolteacher and coach, and she's a social worker, and their incomes total about $65,000 a year.

Their child care expenses decreased substantially when their youngest child started first grade. Then they realized that their oldest child was doing poorly in junior high school. He had learning disabilities, and their local school did not seem to meet his growing emotional and educational needs.

They were faced with a dilemma. They considered moving to a different school district, but everyone else in the family was happy. A move entailed long-term major expenses, readjustments for all, and no assurance of helping their son. Finally, disruptive behavioral problems and constant staying home from school signaled the time to make a solid decision. The parents feared that if it got worse, one or the other would have to stay home from work to supervise the son, who increasingly refused to go to or stay in school. So John and Betty decided to send their teenage son to a competent, though costly, boarding school because it had a fine reputation for teaching children with learning problems. Because their son was not yet fifteen, they claimed a tax credit equal to the applicable percent of work-related child care expense: the room and board costs of the school, not the tuition. They added baby-sitting expenses to that figure and claimed $960 or 20 percent of $4,800 as their tax credit.

Peggy and Sam

Peggy and Sam hired a sleep-in housekeeper to care for their children because each of them had unusually varied work schedules. They realized they had a problem when, after a particularly crazy work week, they had to use two sitters working shifts! When one left at six, another had to cover until either Peggy or Sam arrived home.

What they didn't realize about hiring a housekeeper was that the entire expense of the housekeeper is work-related (even if the worker performs household duties while the children are in school) because the primary purpose of the housekeeper is to care for the well-being of the child(ren) and allow the parents to work.

Peggy and Sam spend far more than the maximum allowable child care expense, and together they earn far more than $28,000, but they claimed this typical tax credit: 20 percent of $4,800. They deducted $960 from their 1983 tax bill.

Sylvia

Sylvia stayed home when the children were little and didn't start working part time until the youngest started first grade. But after the divorce, she realized that she couldn't have the lifestyle she had previously enjoyed on her part-time income, even though her husband paid child support regularly.

Sylvia's boss was pleased to have her on the staff full time, and her income increased accordingly. Her children, aged nine and twelve, asked to stay home alone after school, but Sylvia felt uncomfortable about that. She wanted someone to be there to supervise the quarrels if nothing else. She hired a woman to work each afternoon from three to six o'clock who was willing to do some light housekeeping and start dinner.

During her first summer of full-time employment, Sylvia realized that day camp would be the best solution both for herself and the children. The cost of camp, which was a necessary expense allowing Sylvia to work, and the cost of the housekeeper reached $4,800.

Sylvia's adjusted gross income was less than $20,000 because she claimed the children as dependents but did not have to claim as income the child support her husband contributes. Therefore, Sylvia is eligible to claim 25 percent of the $4,800 based on her adjusted gross income of under $20,000. Her tax credit is $1,200.

What You Can't Do

You may hear about working mothers doing any one of these things, but I think you should be aware that any of them might be challenged by the IRS.

- Your employer pays your sitter's wages directly from the business payroll and reduces your income (and your tax bracket) accordingly.
- You pay a nonprofit or charitable institution for group care, rather than a private nursery school, and deduct the cost as a donation.
- Your employer donates enough money to a private school to cover the cost of your child's "scholarship."
- You pay the sitter off the books and claim group care or out-of-home care for your tax credit.

- Your sitter wants $3 an hour off the books. You want to claim the tax credits, but you need to pay $5 an hour to accumulate the maximum child care expense. The earnings will not raise sitter's taxes, so you strike a deal: you both pay FICA, you meet responsibilities, and she "kicks-back" $1.50 an hour. She ends up with almost $3.50 (minus FICA) an hour and you claim credits.

IRVINA SIEGEL LEW was educated at the College of William and Mary, the Sorbonne, and Adelphi University, where she received her B.A. and M.A. Except for brief intermissions when her three daughters were born, she has taught French and Spanish in the New York City public school system for over twenty years. She is a contributing editor of *Waterway Guide* and a dining contributor to *Nightlife* magazine. Her articles and essays have been published in the *New York Times, Newsday,* and *Baby Talk*. She lives in Bay Shore, New York, with her family.